A Gift For

_____

From

_____

Date

_____

THE
GREATEST
BIBLE
PROMISES

FOR HEALING & COMFORT

SMITH WIGGLESWORTH

WHITAKER
HOUSE

All Scripture quotations are taken from the *King James Version Easy Read Bible*, KJVER®, © 2001, 2007, 2010, 2015 by Whitaker House. Used by permission. All rights reserved.

The Greatest Bible Promises for Healing and Comfort

ISBN: 978-1-62911-870-3
eBook ISBN: 978-1-62911-873-4
Printed in the United States of America
© 2017 by Whitaker House

Whitaker House
1030 Hunt Valley Circle
New Kensington, PA 15068
www.whitakerhouse.com

1 2 3 4 5 6 7 8 9 10 11 **ᵂ** 24 23 22 21 20 19 18 17

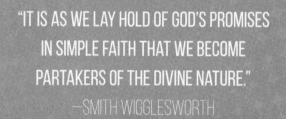

"IT IS AS WE LAY HOLD OF GOD'S PROMISES
IN SIMPLE FAITH THAT WE BECOME
PARTAKERS OF THE DIVINE NATURE."
—SMITH WIGGLESWORTH

CONTENTS

CHAPTER 2: HE TOOK OUR INFIRMITIES

CHAPTER 3: FAITH THAT DELIVERS

CHAPTER 4: WORDS OF LIFE

CHAPTER 5: JESUS' LIFE IN YOU

CHAPTER 6: THE LORD HEALS

CHAPTER 7: COMFORT FOR EVERY NEED

A WORD FROM THE EDITOR

The Greatest Bible Promises is a collection of God's promises in Scripture, from the *King James Version Easy Read Bible* (KJVER), combined with beloved quotes from the various writings of the Apostle of Faith, Smith Wigglesworth (1859–1947).

An encounter with Smith Wigglesworth was an unforgettable experience. This seems to be the universal reaction of all who knew him or heard him speak. Wigglesworth was a simple yet remarkable man who was used by God in extraordinary ways. He had a contagious and inspiring faith. Under his ministry, thousands of people came to salvation, committed themselves to a deeper faith in Christ, received the baptism in the Holy Spirit, and were miraculously healed. The power that brought these kinds of results was the presence of the Holy Spirit, who filled Smith Wigglesworth and used him in bringing the good news of the gospel to people all over the world. Wigglesworth gave glory to God for everything that was accomplished through his ministry, and he wanted people to understand his work only in this context, because his sole desire was that people would see Jesus and not himself.

It is our hope that by reading Wigglesworth's words of wisdom and inspiration combined with the wonderful promises found in Scripture, you will truly experience the divine presence of our miraculous God and take to heart one of Wigglesworth's favorite sayings: "Only believe!"

LET ME SAY A WORD TO YOUR HEARTS...

Blessed be God, even the Father of our Lord Jesus Christ,
the Father of mercies, and the God of all comfort.
—2 Corinthians 1:3

Every trial is a blessing. There have been times when I have been hard-pressed through dire circumstances, and it seemed as if a dozen steamrollers were going over me, but I have found that the hardest things are just lifting places into the grace of God. We have such a lovely Jesus. He always proves Himself to be such a mighty Deliverer. He never fails to plan the best things for us.

⁓

We must understand that God, in these times, wants to bring us into perfect life so that we never, under any circumstances, need to go outside of His Word for anything. A broken spirit, a tried life, and being driven into a corner as if some strange thing had happened—these are surely the ways in which we to get to know the way of God.

〰

God has told us that all things will work together for our good. (See Romans 8:28.) God has said that we will be the "children of the Highest" and that we will be the "salt of the earth." God has declared all that in His Word, and you will never reach those beatitudes if you are holding on to the lower things of this world; they will keep you down.

〰

How am I to have all the treasures of heaven and all the treasures of God? Not by getting my eyes on the things that are seen, for they will fade away. I must get my eyes on the things that are not seen, for they will remain as long as God reigns.

〰

If you have lost your hunger for God, if you do not have a cry for more of God, you are missing the plan. A cry must come up from us that cannot be satisfied with anything but God. He wants to give us the vision of the prize ahead that is something higher than we have ever attained. If you ever stop at any point, pick up at the place where you have left off, and begin again under the refining light and power of heaven. God will meet you. And while He will bring you to a consciousness of your own frailty and to a brokenness of spirit, your faith will lay hold of Him and all the divine resources.

His light and compassion will be manifested through you, and He will send the rain.

~

Believe that He is in you. Believe that He is almightiness. Believe that He is all fullness. Then let yourself go until He is on the throne of your heart. Let everything submit itself to God's throne and the King. Yield yourself unto Him in so sublime a position that He is in perfect order over everything. Let God have His perfect way through you. If you will let go, God will take hold and keep you up.

~

Come on a little nearer now. There are opportunities. God has the right-of-way to the heart and life to bring them to a place where opportunities are made for the possibility of being accomplished. I am realizing that God must impress upon your heart around you, wherever you are, that He has an opportunity for you today. It will stand right in front of you, and by that means you will be brought into a place where you will convince the people because God is there. Without the shadow of a doubt, the Word of God is effective and destroying, and it brings about perfect life.

—*Smith Wigglesworth*

"JESUS CAME TO SET US FREE FROM SIN, AND TO FREE US FROM SICKNESS, SO THAT WE WILL GO FORTH IN THE POWER OF THE SPIRIT AND MINISTER TO THE NEEDY, SICK, AND AFFLICTED. THROUGH THE REVELATION OF THE WORD OF GOD, WE FIND THAT DIVINE HEALING IS SOLELY FOR THE GLORY OF GOD, AND THAT SALVATION IS WALKING IN NEWNESS OF LIFE SO THAT WE ARE INHABITED BY ANOTHER, EVEN GOD."

—SMITH WIGGLESWORTH

1

HEALING PROMISES FOR VICTORY

ABORTION

Lo, children are a heritage of the Lord: and the fruit of the womb is His reward. PSALM 127:3

Wash you, make you clean; put away the evil of your doings from before My eyes; cease to do evil; learn to do well; seek judgment, relieve the oppressed, judge the fatherless, plead for the widow. Come now, and let us reason together, says the Lord: though your sins be as scarlet, they shall be as white as snow; though they be red like crimson, they shall be as wool. ISAIAH 1:16–18

Can a woman forget her sucking child, that she should not have compassion on the son of her womb? yea, they may forget, yet will I not forget you. ISAIAH 49:15

Before I formed you in the belly I knew you; and before you came forth out of the womb I sanctified you, and I ordained you a prophet to the nations. JEREMIAH 1:5

ABUSE

I sought the LORD, and He heard me, and delivered me from all my fears. They looked to Him, and were lightened: and their faces were not ashamed. PSALM 34:4–5

Behold, how good and how pleasant it is for brethren to dwell together in unity! PSALM 133:1

A man that has friends must show himself friendly: and there is a friend that sticks closer than a brother. PROVERBS 18:24

Trust you in the LORD for ever: for in the LORD JEHOVAH is everlasting strength: For he brings down them that dwell on high; the lofty city, He lays it low; He lays it low, even to the ground; He brings it even to the dust. ISAIAH 26:4–5

He that receives you receives Me, and he that receives Me receives Him that sent Me. MATTHEW 10:40

This is My commandment, That you love one another, as I have loved you. Greater love has no man than this, that a man lay down his life for his friends. JOHN 15:12–13

Then Peter opened his mouth, and said, Of a truth I perceive that God is no respecter of persons: but in every nation he that fears Him, and works righteousness, is accepted with Him.

ACTS 10:34–35

But the fruit of the Spirit is love, joy, peace, longsuffering, gentleness, goodness, faith, meekness, temperance: against such there is no law.   GALATIANS 5:22–23

For He is our peace, who has made both one, and has broken down the middle wall of partition between us. EPHESIANS 2:14

Husbands, love your wives, even as Christ also loved the church, and gave Himself for it.   EPHESIANS 5:25

And let us consider one another to provoke to love and to good works.   HEBREWS 10:24

And, you fathers, provoke not your children to wrath: but bring them up in the nurture and admonition of the Lord.

EPHESIANS 6:4

If we confess our sins, He is faithful and just to forgive us our sins, and to cleanse us from all unrighteousness.   1 JOHN 1:9

INSIGHTS ON FAITH FROM SMITH WIGGLESWORTH

There is power to overcome everything in the world through the name of Jesus. I am looking forward to a wonderful union through the name of Jesus…. There is no other name under heaven given among men by which we must be saved.

⌁

If you are definite with Him, you will never go away disappointed. The divine life will flow into you, and instantaneously you will be delivered. This Jesus is just the same today, and He says to you, "I am willing; be cleansed." He has an overflowing cup for you, a fullness of life. He will meet you in your absolute helplessness.

⌁

There are times when everything seems as black as midnight, and there is nothing left but confidence in God. What you must do is have the devotion and confidence to believe that He will not fail, and cannot fail. You will never get anywhere if you depend on your feelings. There is something a thousand times better than feelings, and it is the powerful Word of God.

ALCOHOL

Wine is a mocker, strong drink is raging: and whosoever is deceived thereby is not wise.   PROVERBS 20:1

Woe to them that rise up early in the morning, that they may follow strong drink; that continue until night, till wine inflame them!   ISAIAH 5:11

Know you not that the unrighteous shall not inherit the kingdom of God? Be not deceived: neither fornicators, nor idolaters, nor adulterers, nor effeminate, nor abusers of themselves with mankind, nor thieves, nor covetous, nor drunkards, nor revilers, nor extortioners, shall inherit the kingdom of God. And such were some of you: but you are washed, but you are sanctified, but you are justified in the name of the Lord Jesus, and by the Spirit of our God.   1 CORINTHIANS 6:9–11

Envyings, murders, drunkenness, revellings, and such like: of the which I tell you before, as I have also told you in time past, that they which do such things shall not inherit the kingdom of God.
GALATIANS 5:21

And be not drunk with wine, wherein is excess; but be filled with the Spirit.   EPHESIANS 5:18

ANGER

For His anger endures but a moment; in His favor is life: weeping may endure for a night, but joy comes in the morning.

PSALM 30:5

The LORD is gracious, and full of compassion; slow to anger, and of great mercy.

PSALM 145:8

He that is slow to wrath is of great understanding: but he that is hasty of spirit exalts folly.

PROVERBS 14:29

The discretion of a man defers his anger; and it is his glory to pass over a transgression.

PROVERBS 19:11

If your enemy be hungry, give him bread to eat; and if he be thirsty, give him water to drink: for you shall heap coals of fire upon his head, and the LORD shall reward you.

PROVERBS 25:21–22

Dearly beloved, avenge not yourselves, but rather give place to wrath: for it is written, Vengeance is Mine; I will repay, says the Lord. Therefore if your enemy hunger, feed him; if he thirst, give him drink: for in so doing you shall heap coals of fire on his head. Be not overcome of evil, but overcome evil with good.

ROMANS 12:19–21

ANXIETY

And He said, My presence shall go with you, and I will give you rest. EXODUS 33:14

The LORD will give strength to His people; the LORD will bless His people with peace. PSALM 29:11

Commit your way to the LORD; trust also in Him; and He shall bring it to pass. And He shall bring forth your righteousness as the light, and your judgment as the noonday. PSALM 37:5–6

In the day of my trouble I will call upon You: for You will answer me. PSALM 86:7

They that trust in the LORD shall be as mount Zion, which cannot be removed, but abides for ever. PSALM 125:1

Therefore I say to you, Take no thought for your life, what you shall eat, or what you shall drink; nor yet for your body, what you shall put on. Is not the life more than meat, and the body than raiment? Behold the fowls of the air: for they sow not, neither do they reap, nor gather into barns; yet your heavenly Father feeds them. Are you not much better than they? MATTHEW 6:25–26

INSIGHTS ON FAITH FROM SMITH WIGGLESWORTH

Every trial is a blessing. There have been times when I have been hard-pressed through circumstances, and it seemed as if a dozen steamrollers were going over me, but I have found that the hardest things are just lifting places into the grace of God. We have such a lovely Jesus. He always proves Himself to be such a mighty Deliverer. He never fails to plan the best things for us.

God has a plan of healing. It is along the lines of perfect confidence in Him. The confidence comes not from our much speaking; it comes from our fellowship with Him. There is a wonderful fellowship with Jesus. The chief thing is to be sure that we take time for communion with Him.

Our God is real, and He has saving and healing power today. Our Jesus is just the same *"yesterday, today, and forever"* (Hebrews 13:8). He saves and heals today just as of old, and He wants to be your Savior and your Healer.

ANXIETY

And He said to His disciples, Therefore I say to you, Take no thought for your life, what you shall eat; neither for the body, what you shall put on. The life is more than meat, and the body is more than raiment.   LUKE 12:22–23

Watch you, stand fast in the faith, quit you like men, be strong.
1 CORINTHIANS 16:13

That He would grant you, according to the riches of His glory, to be strengthened with might by His Spirit in the inner man; that Christ may dwell in your hearts by faith; that you, being rooted and grounded in love, may be able to comprehend with all saints what is the breadth, and length, and depth, and height; and to know the love of Christ, which passes knowledge, that you might be filled with all the fullness of God.   EPHESIANS 3:16–19

Be careful for nothing; but in every thing by prayer and supplication with thanksgiving let your requests be made known to God.
PHILIPPIANS 4:6

Casting all your care upon Him; for He cares for you.
1 PETER 5:7

BATTLE FOR YOUR MIND

Then said Jesus to those Jews which believed on Him, If you continue in My word, then are you My disciples indeed; and you shall know the truth, and the truth shall make you free.

JOHN 8:31–32

Jesus says to him, I am the way, the truth, and the life: no man comes to the Father, but by Me. JOHN 14:6

Nay, in all these things we are more than conquerors through Him that loved us. ROMANS 8:37

And be not conformed to this world: but be you transformed by the renewing of your mind, that you may prove what is that good, and acceptable, and perfect, will of God. ROMANS 12:2

For who has known the mind of the Lord, that he may instruct Him? but we have the mind of Christ. 1 CORINTHIANS 2:16

For the weapons of our warfare are not carnal, but mighty through God to the pulling down of strong holds. Casting down imaginations, and every high thing that exalts itself against the knowledge of God, and bringing into captivity every thought to the obedience of Christ. 2 CORINTHIANS 10:4–5

Be careful for nothing; but in every thing by prayer and supplication with thanksgiving let your requests be made known to God. And the peace of God, which passes all understanding, shall keep your hearts and minds through Christ Jesus. Finally, brethren, whatsoever things are true, whatsoever things are honest, whatsoever things are just, whatsoever things are pure, whatsoever things are lovely, whatsoever things are of good report; if there be any virtue, and if there be any praise, think on these things.

PHILIPPIANS 4:6–8

Who has delivered us from the power of darkness, and has translated us into the kingdom of His dear Son.   COLOSSIANS 1:13

Submit yourselves therefore to God. Resist the devil, and he will flee from you.   JAMES 4:7

As free, and not using your liberty for a cloak of maliciousness, but as the servants of God.   1 PETER 2:16

Little children, let no man deceive you: He that does righteousness is righteous, even as He is righteous.   1 JOHN 3:7

INSIGHTS ON FAITH FROM SMITH WIGGLESWORTH

Are you oppressed? Cry out to God. It is always good for people to cry out. You may have to cry out. The Holy Spirit and the Word of God will bring to light every hidden, unclean thing that must be revealed. There is always a place of deliverance when you let God search out what is spoiling and marring your life.

God is compassionate and says, *"Seek the LORD while He may be found"* (Isaiah 55:6). He has further stated, *"Whoever calls on the name of the Lord shall be saved"* (Acts 2:21). Seek Him now; call on His name right now. There is forgiveness, healing, redemption, deliverance—everything you need right here and now, and that which will satisfy you throughout eternity.

God is greater than your heart, greater than your circumstances, greater than the thing that holds you. God will deliver you if you dare to believe Him.

BITTERNESS

A soft answer turns away wrath: but grievous words stir up anger. PROVERBS 15:1

Nay not you, I will recompense evil; but wait on the LORD, and He shall save you. PROVERBS 20:22

And when you stand praying, forgive, if you have anything against any: that your Father also which is in heaven may forgive you your trespasses. MARK 11:25

Bless them which persecute you: bless, and curse not. ROMANS 12:14

Recompense to no man evil for evil. Provide things honest in the sight of all men. ROMANS 12:17

Let all bitterness, and wrath, and anger, and clamor, and evil speaking, be put away from you, with all malice: and be you kind one to another, tenderhearted, forgiving one another, even as God for Christ's sake has forgiven you. EPHESIANS 4:31–32

Fulfill you my joy, that you be likeminded, having the same love, being of one accord, of one mind. Let nothing be done through strife or vainglory; but in lowliness of mind let each esteem other better than themselves. Look not every man on his own things, but every man also on the things of others.

PHILIPPIANS 2:2–4

But now you also put off all these; anger, wrath, malice, blasphemy, filthy communication out of your mouth.

COLOSSIANS 3:8

Follow peace with all men, and holiness, without which no man shall see the Lord: looking diligently lest any man fail of the grace of God; lest any root of bitterness springing up trouble you, and thereby many be defiled.   HEBREWS 12:14–15

Out of the same mouth proceeds blessing and cursing. My brethren, these things ought not so to be.   JAMES 3:10

For even hereto were you called: because Christ also suffered for us, leaving us an example, that you should follow His steps: who did no sin, neither was guile found in his mouth.

1 PETER 2:21–22

BONDAGE

A righteous man falling down before the wicked is as a troubled fountain, and a corrupt spring. PROVERBS 25:26

Awake, awake, put on strength, O arm of the LORD; awake, as in the ancient days, in the generations of old. Are You not it that has cut Rahab, and wounded the dragon? ISAIAH 51:9

And be not conformed to this world: but be you transformed by the renewing of your mind, that you may prove what is that good, and acceptable, and perfect, will of God. ROMANS 12:2

There has no temptation taken you but such as is common to man: but God is faithful, who will not suffer you to be tempted above that you are able; but will with the temptation also make a way to escape, that you may be able to bear it.
1 CORINTHIANS 10:13

Stand fast therefore in the liberty wherewith Christ has made us free, and be not entangled again with the yoke of bondage.
GALATIANS 5:1

Submit yourselves therefore to God. Resist the devil, and he will flee from you. JAMES 4:7

INSIGHTS ON FAITH FROM SMITH WIGGLESWORTH

Allow God to touch your flesh. He has given life to your spirit. Allow Him to reign, for He will reign until all is subdued. He is King in your life and is preeminent over your affections, your will, your desires, your plans. He rules as Lord of Hosts over you, in you, and through you, to chasten you and bring you to the perfection of your desired haven. *"Christ in you [is] the hope of glory"* (Colossians 1:27).

❧

What then shall we say to these things? If God is for us, who can be against us?… Who shall separate us from the love of Christ? Shall tribulation, or distress, or persecution, or famine, or nakedness, or peril, or sword?… Yet in all these things we are more than conquerors through Him who loved us.

❧

All things are wonderful with our wonderful Jesus. If you would dare rest your all upon Him, things would take place, and He would change the whole situation. In a moment, through the name of Jesus, a new order of things can be brought in.

CONFIDENCE

The LORD is my light and my salvation; whom shall I fear? the LORD is the strength of my life; of whom shall I be afraid? When the wicked, even my enemies and my foes, came upon me to eat up my flesh, they stumbled and fell. Though a host should encamp against me, my heart shall not fear: though war should rise against me, in this will I be confident.   PSALM 27:1–3

For the LORD shall be your confidence, and shall keep your foot from being taken.   PROVERBS 3:26

In the fear of the LORD is strong confidence: and his children shall have a place of refuge.   PROVERBS 14:26

Fear you not; for I am with you: be not dismayed; for I am Your God: I will strengthen you; yea, I will help you; yea, I will uphold you with the right hand of My righteousness.   ISAIAH 41:10

Now the God of hope fill you with all joy and peace in believing, that you may abound in hope, through the power of the Holy Ghost.   ROMANS 15:13

So that we may boldly say, The Lord is my helper, and I will not fear what man shall do to me.   HEBREWS 13:6

CONFUSION

Evil men understand not judgment: but they that seek the Lord *understand all things.* Proverbs 28:5

No weapon that is formed against you shall prosper; and every tongue that shall rise against you in judgment you shall condemn. This is the heritage of the servants of the Lord, *and their righteousness is of Me, says the* Lord. Isaiah 54:17

I the Lord *search the heart, I try the reins, even to give every man according to his ways, and according to the fruit of his doings.* Jeremiah 17:10

But the Comforter, which is the Holy Ghost, whom the Father will send in My name, He shall teach you all things, and bring all things to your remembrance, whatsoever I have said to you. John 14:26

However when He, the Spirit of truth, is come, He will guide you into all truth: for He shall not speak of Himself; but whatsoever He shall hear, that shall He speak: and He will show you things to come. John 16:13

For God is not the author of confusion, but of peace, as in all churches of the saints. 1 Corinthians 14:33

Finally, brethren, whatsoever things are true, whatsoever things are honest, whatsoever things are just, whatsoever things are pure, whatsoever things are lovely, whatsoever things are of good report; if there be any virtue, and if there be any praise, think on these things. Those things, which you have both learned, and received, and heard, and seen in me, do: and the God of peace shall be with you. PHILIPPIANS 4:8–9

Casting all your care upon him; for He cares for you.
1 PETER 5:7

Be sober, be vigilant; because your adversary the devil, as a roaring lion, walks about, seeking whom he may devour.
1 PETER 5:8

Beloved, believe not every spirit, but try the spirits whether they are of God: because many false prophets are gone out into the world. 1 JOHN 4:1

INSIGHTS ON FAITH FROM SMITH WIGGLESWORTH

It is necessary to discover the meaning of these wonderful verses. There is nothing that will bring you such confidence as a life that is well pleasing to God. When Daniel's life pleased God, he could ask to be protected in the lions' den. But you cannot ask with confidence until there is a perfect union between you and God, as there was always a perfect union between God and Jesus. The foundation is confidence in and loyalty to God.

⌣

Do you not see that the words of the Master are the instruction of faith? It is impossible for anything that Jesus says to miss. All His words are spirit and life. (See John 6:63.) If you will only have faith in Him, you will find that every word that God gives is life. You cannot be in close contact with Him and receive His Word in simple faith without feeling the effect of it in your body, as well as in your spirit and soul.

CONTENTMENT

Rest in the LORD, and wait patiently for him: fret not yourself because of him who prospers in his way, because of the man who brings wicked devices to pass. Cease from anger, and forsake wrath: fret not yourself in any wise to do evil. For evildoers shall be cut off: but those that wait upon the LORD, they shall inherit the earth.   PSALM 37:7–9

A sound heart is the life of the flesh: but envy the rottenness of the bones.   PROVERBS 14:30

A merry heart makes a cheerful countenance: but by sorrow of the heart the spirit is broken.   PROVERBS 15:13

All the days of the afflicted are evil: but he that is of a merry heart has a continual feast.   PROVERBS 15:15

But godliness with contentment is great gain.   1 TIMOTHY 6:6

Let your conversation be without covetousness; and be content with such things as you have: for He has said, I will never leave you, nor forsake you.   HEBREWS 13:5

COURAGE

Have not I commanded you? Be strong and of a good courage; be not afraid, neither be you dismayed: for the LORD your God is with you wherever you go. JOSHUA 1:9

I will love You, O LORD, my strength. The LORD is my rock, and my fortress, and my deliverer; my God, my strength, in whom I will trust; my buckler, and the horn of my salvation, and my high tower. PSALM 18:1–2

Wait on the LORD: be of good courage, and he shall strengthen your heart: wait, I say, on the LORD. PSALM 27:14

Fear you not; for I am with you: be not dismayed; for I am Your God: I will strengthen you; yea, I will help you; yea, I will uphold you with the right hand of My righteousness. ISAIAH 41:10

When you pass through the waters, I will be with you; and through the rivers, they shall not overflow you: when thou walk through the fire, you shall not be burned; neither shall the flame kindle upon you. For I am the LORD your God, the Holy One of Israel, your Savior: I gave Egypt for your ransom, Ethiopia and Seba for you. Since you were precious in My sight, you have been honorable, and I have loved you: therefore will I give men for you, and people for your life. ISAIAH 43:2–4

But Christ as a son over His own house; whose house are we, if we hold fast the confidence and the rejoicing of the hope firm to the end.   HEBREWS 3:6

For they verily for a few days chastened us after their own pleasure; but he for our profit, that we might be partakers of his holiness. Now no chastening for the present seems to be joyous, but grievous: nevertheless afterward it yields the peaceable fruit of righteousness unto them which are exercised thereby. Wherefore lift up the hands which hang down, and the feeble knees; and make straight paths for your feet, lest that which is lame be turned out of the way; but let it rather be healed.   HEBREWS 12:10–13

Beloved, think it not strange concerning the fiery trial which is to try you, as though some strange thing happened to you: but rejoice, inasmuch as you are partakers of Christ's sufferings; that, when His glory shall be revealed, you may be glad also with exceeding joy.   1 PETER 4:12–13

And let us not be weary in well doing: for in due season we shall reap, if we faint not.   GALATIANS 6:9

INSIGHTS ON FAITH FROM SMITH WIGGLESWORTH

Do you keep in mind how God has been gracious in the past? God has done wonderful things for all of us. If we keep these things in mind, we will become "strong in faith."

⌒

"He who believes in Me"—the essence of divine life is in us by faith. To the one who believes, it will come to pass. We become supernatural by the power of God. If you believe, the power of the Enemy cannot stand, for God's Word is against him. Jesus gives us His Word to make faith effective. If you can believe in your heart, you begin to speak whatever you desire, and whatever you dare to say is done. You will have whatever you say after you believe in your heart.

⌒

God's Word never fails. He will always heal you if you dare to believe Him. Men are searching everywhere today for things with which they can heal themselves, and they ignore the fact that the Balm of Gilead is within easy reach.

DECEIT

Judge me, O God, and plead my cause against an ungodly nation: O deliver me from the deceitful and unjust man.   PSALM 43:1

He that works deceit shall not dwell within My house: he that tells lies shall not tarry in My sight.   PSALM 101:7

Deliver my soul, O LORD, from lying lips, and from a deceitful tongue.   PSALM 120:2

These six things does the LORD hate: yea, seven are an abomination to him: a proud look, a lying tongue, and hands that shed innocent blood, a heart that devises wicked imaginations, feet that be swift in running to mischief, a false witness that speaks lies, and he that sows discord among brethren.   PROVERBS 6:16–19

Let no man deceive you with vain words: for because of these things comes the wrath of God upon the children of disobedience.   EPHESIANS 5:6

DEFEAT

He brought me up also out of a horrible pit, out of the miry clay, and set my feet upon a rock, and established my goings. And He has put a new song in my mouth, even praise to our God: many shall see it, and fear, and shall trust in the LORD.

PSALM 40:2–3

For a just man falls seven times, and rises up again: but the wicked shall fall into mischief. PROVERBS 24:16

For I am the LORD, I change not; therefore you sons of Jacob are not consumed. MALACHI 3:6

If the world hate you, you know that it hated Me before it hated you. JOHN 15:18

Dearly beloved, avenge not yourselves, but rather give place to wrath: for it is written, Vengeance is Mine; I will repay, says the Lord. ROMANS 12:19

For which cause we faint not; but though our outward man perish, yet the inward man is renewed day by day.

2 CORINTHIANS 4:16

DELIVERANCE

And he said, The LORD is my rock, and my fortress, and my deliverer.   2 SAMUEL 22:2

For You will light my candle: the LORD my God will enlighten my darkness. For by You I have run through a troop; and by my God have I leaped over a wall.   PSALM 18: 28–29

I will bless the LORD at all times: His praise shall continually be in my mouth. My soul shall make her boast in the LORD: the humble shall hear thereof, and be glad. O magnify the LORD with me, and let us exalt His name together. I sought the LORD, and He heard me, and delivered me from all my fears. They looked to Him, and were lightened: and their faces were not ashamed. This poor man cried, and the LORD heard him, and saved him out of all his troubles.   PSALM 34:1–6

Many are the afflictions of the righteous: but the LORD delivers him out of them all. He keeps all his bones: not one of them is broken. Evil shall slay the wicked: and they that hate the righteous shall be desolate. The LORD redeems the soul of His servants: and none of them that trust in Him shall be desolate.

PSALM 34:19–22

An ungodly man digs up evil: and in his lips there is as a burning fire.   PROVERBS 16:27

INSIGHTS ON FAITH FROM SMITH WIGGLESWORTH

God is speaking to us, every one of us, and trying to get us to leave the shoreline. There is only one place where we can get the mind and will of God; it is alone with God. If we look to anybody else, we cannot get it. If we seek to save ourselves, we will never reach the place where we will be able to bind and loose. There is a close companionship between you and Jesus that nobody knows about, where every day you have to choose or refuse.

~

God declared Himself to be mightier than every opposing power when He cast out the powers of darkness from heaven. I want you to know that the same power that cast Satan out of heaven dwells in every person who is born of God. If you would only realize this, you would *"reign in life"* (Romans 5:17).

"THERE ARE TWO THINGS THAT ARE CERTAIN, AND THERE IS A THIRD THING THAT IS MORE VALUABLE THAN EITHER OF THE FIRST TWO. ONE IS THAT THE DEVIL DOESN'T LET YOU FORGET YOUR SINS; THE SECOND IS THAT YOU NEVER FORGET THEM; AND THE THIRD IS THAT GOD HAS FORGOTTEN THEM. THE QUESTION IS WHETHER WE ARE GOING TO BELIEVE GOD, THE DEVIL, OR OURSELVES. GOD SAYS THAT OUR SINS ARE PASSED, CLEANSED, GONE!"

—SMITH WIGGLESWORTH

2

HE TOOK OUR INFIRMITIES

DEPRESSION

For you are my lamp, O LORD: and the LORD will lighten my darkness.   2 SAMUEL 22:29

I said in my haste, I am cut off from before Your eyes: nevertheless You heard the voice of my supplications when I cried to You. O love the LORD, all you His saints: for the LORD preserves the faithful, and plentifully rewards the proud doer. Be of good courage, and He shall strengthen your heart, all you that hope in the LORD.   PSALM 31:22–24

I sought the LORD, and He heard me, and delivered me from all my fears.   PSALM 34:4

The steps of a good man are ordered by the LORD: and He delights in his way. Though he fall, he shall not be utterly cast down: for the LORD upholds him with His hand.   PSALM 37:23–24

Hear me speedily, O LORD: my spirit fails: hide not Your face from me, lest I be like to them that go down into the pit. Cause me to hear Your lovingkindness in the morning; for in You do I trust: cause me to know the way wherein I should walk; for I lift up my soul to You. PSALM 143:7–8

You will keep him in perfect peace, whose mind is stayed on You: because he trusts in You. ISAIAH 26:3

He gives power to the faint; and to them that have no might he increases strength. ISAIAH 40:29

Even the youths shall faint and be weary, and the young men shall utterly fall: but they that wait upon the LORD shall renew their strength; they shall mount up with wings as eagles; they shall run, and not be weary; and they shall walk, and not faint. ISAIAH 40:30–31

For I have satiated the weary soul, and I have replenished every sorrowful soul. JEREMIAH 31:25

I cried by reason of my affliction to the LORD, and He heard me; out of the belly of hell cried I, and You heard my voice. JONAH 2:2

Behold the fowls of the air: for they sow not, neither do they reap, nor gather into barns; yet your heavenly Father feeds them. Are you not much better than they? MATTHEW 6:26

DISAPPOINTMENT

Behold, the eye of the Lord *is upon them that fear Him, upon them that hope in His mercy.* Psalm 33:18

Trust in Him at all times; you people, pour out your heart before him: God is a refuge for us. Psalm 62:8

I cried to God with my voice, even to God with my voice; and He gave ear to me. Psalm 77:1

A merry heart does good like a medicine: but a broken spirit dries the bones. Proverbs 17:22

For their redeemer is mighty; He shall plead their cause with you. Proverbs 23:11

In the day of prosperity be joyful, but in the day of adversity consider: God also has set the one over against the other, to the end that man should find nothing after him. Ecclesiastes 7:14

INSIGHTS ON FAITH FROM SMITH WIGGLESWORTH

If we dare come believing, God will heal; God will restore and will lift the burden and will wake us up to real, overcoming faith. Look up; take courage! Jesus has shaken the foundations of death and darkness. He fights for you, and there is none like Him. He is the great I Am. His name is above every name. As we believe, we are lifted into a place of rest, a place of conformity to Him.

If you went to see a doctor, the more you told him, the more he would know. But when you come to Doctor Jesus, He knows everything from the beginning, and He never gives you the wrong medicine.

God wants to spread forth His wings and show that He is able, He is Almightiness, and He is able to preserve what we have committed to Him, because He is our Lord. He is not only our Creator, but also the One who preserves us. He has not only redeemed me, but He is also preserving me. I see I cannot do any of these things by myself, but He has made it possible that if I believe, He will do it.

DISCOURAGEMENT

Blessed are they that mourn: for they shall be comforted.

MATTHEW 5:4

Blessed are you that hunger now: for you shall be filled. Blessed are you that weep now: for you shall laugh.   LUKE 6:21

Likewise the Spirit also helps our infirmities: for we know not what we should pray for as we ought: but the Spirit itself makes intercession for us with groanings which cannot be uttered.

ROMANS 8:26

We are troubled on every side, yet not distressed; we are perplexed, but not in despair.   2 CORINTHIANS 4:8

Knowing that He which raised up the Lord Jesus shall raise up us also by Jesus, and shall present us with you.

2 CORINTHIANS 4:14

For our light affliction, which is but for a moment, works for us a far more exceeding and eternal weight of glory; while we look not at the things which are seen, but at the things which are not seen: for the things which are seen are temporal; but the things which are not seen are eternal.   2 CORINTHIANS 4:17–18

DOUBT

Fear you not; for I am with you: be not dismayed; for I am Your God: I will strengthen you; yea, I will help you; yea, I will uphold you with the right hand of My righteousness.   Isaiah 41:10

For I know the thoughts that I think toward you, says the LORD, thoughts of peace, and not of evil, to give you an expected end. Then shall you call upon Me, and you shall go and pray to Me, and I will hearken to you. And you shall seek Me, and find Me, when you shall search for Me with all your heart.

Jeremiah 29:11–13

And He says to them, Why are you fearful, O you of little faith? Then He arose, and rebuked the winds and the sea; and there was a great calm.   Matthew 8:26

And immediately Jesus stretched forth His hand, and caught him, and said to him, O you of little faith, wherefore did you doubt?

Matthew 14:31

Jesus answered and said to them, Verily I say to you, If you have faith, and doubt not, you shall not only do this which is done to the fig tree, but also if you shall say to this mountain, Be you removed, and be you cast into the sea; it shall be done.   Matthew 21:21

And I say to you, Ask, and it shall be given you; seek, and you shall find; knock, and it shall be opened to you. For every one that asks receives; and he that seeks finds; and to him that knocks it shall be opened. If a son shall ask bread of any of you that is a father, will he give him a stone? or if he ask a fish, will he for a fish give him a serpent? Or if he shall ask an egg, will he offer him a scorpion? If you then, being evil, know how to give good gifts to your children: how much more shall your heavenly Father give the Holy Spirit to them that ask Him? LUKE 11:9–13

But without faith it is impossible to please Him: for he that comes to God must believe that He is, and that He is a rewarder of them that diligently seek Him. HEBREWS 11:6

If any of you lack wisdom, let him ask of God, that gives to all men liberally, and upbraids not; and it shall be given him. But let him ask in faith, nothing wavering. For he that wavers is like a wave of the sea driven with the wind and tossed. For let not that man think that he shall receive any thing of the Lord. A double minded man is unstable in all his ways. JAMES 1:5–8

INSIGHTS ON FAITH FROM SMITH WIGGLESWORTH

Jesus sends His healing power and brings His restoring grace, and so there is nothing to fear. The only thing that is wrong is your wrong conception of the mightiness of His redemption.

He was wounded so that He might be touched with a feeling of your infirmities. He took your flesh and laid it upon the cross so that *"he might destroy him that had the power of death, that is, the devil; and deliver them who through fear of death were all their lifetime subject to bondage"* (Hebrews 2:14–15).

◡

Beloved, I wonder how much you want to take away today. You could not carry it if it were an actual substance. But there is something about the grace and the power and the blessings of God that can be carried, no matter how big they are. Oh, what a Savior! What a place we are in, by grace, that He may come in to commune with us! He is willing to say to every heart, *"Peace, be still!"* (Mark 4:39), and to every weak body, "Be strong."

◡

There is no such thing as the Lord's not meeting your need. There are no ifs or mays; His promises are all shalls. *"All things are possible to him who believes"* (Mark 9:23). Oh, the name of Jesus! There is power in that name to meet every human need.

FAILURE

And David said to Solomon his son, Be strong and of good courage, and do it: fear not, nor be dismayed: for the Lord *God, even my God, will be with you; He will not fail you, nor forsake you, until you have finished all the work for the service of the house of the* Lord. 1 Chronicles 28:20

Cast your burden upon the Lord, *and He shall sustain you: He shall never allow the righteous to be moved.* Psalm 55:22

My flesh and my heart fails: but God is the strength of my heart, and my portion for ever. Psalm 73:26

For a just man falls seven times, and rises up again: but the wicked shall fall into mischief. Proverbs 24:16

It is of the Lord's *mercies that we are not consumed, because His compassions fail not. They are new every morning: great is Your faithfulness.* Lamentations 3:22–23

For all things are for your sakes, that the abundant grace might through the thanksgiving of many redound to the glory of God. For which cause we faint not; but though our outward man perish, yet the inward man is renewed day by day.

2 Corinthians 4:15–16

FEAR

Yea, though I walk through the valley of the shadow of death, I will fear no evil: for You are with me; Your rod and Your staff they comfort me. You prepare a table before me in the presence of my enemies: You anoint my head with oil; my cup runs over.

PSALM 23:4–5

He shall cover you with His feathers, and under His wings shall you trust: His truth shall be your shield and buckler. You shall not be afraid for the terror by night; nor for the arrow that flies by day; nor for the pestilence that walks in darkness; nor for the destruction that wastes at noonday.

PSALM 91:4–6

The fear of man brings a snare: but whoso puts his trust in the LORD *shall be safe.*

PROVERBS 29:25

When you lie down, you shall not be afraid: yea, you shall lie down, and your sleep shall be sweet.

PROVERBS 3:24

Be not afraid of sudden fear, neither of the desolation of the wicked, when it comes. For the LORD *shall be your confidence, and shall keep your foot from being taken.*

PROVERBS 3:25–26

INSIGHTS ON FAITH FROM SMITH WIGGLESWORTH

You must cease to be. That is a difficult thing for you and me, but it is no trouble at all when you are in the hands of the Potter. You are only wrong when you are kicking. You are all right when you are still and He is forming you afresh. So let Him form you afresh today and make another vessel so that you will stand the stress.

❧

You can receive something in three minutes that you can carry with you into glory. What do you want? Is anything too hard for God? God can meet you now. God sees inwardly. He knows all about you. Nothing is hidden from Him, and He can satisfy the soul and give you a spring of eternal blessing that will carry you right through.

❧

Many can testify to the day and hour when they were delivered from sickness by a supernatural power. Some would have passed away with influenza if God had not intervened, but God stepped in with a new revelation, showing us we are born from above, born by a new power, God dwelling in us and superseding the old. *"If you ask anything in My name, I will do it"* (John 14:14).

FEAR

And it shall come to pass in the day that the LORD shall give you rest from your sorrow, and from your fear, and from the hard bondage wherein you were made to serve.   ISAIAH 14:3

I, even I, am He that comforts you: who are you, that you should be afraid of a man that shall die, and of the son of man which shall be made as grass.   ISAIAH 51:12

And He said to them, Why are you so fearful? how is it that you have no faith?   MARK 4:40

Fear not, little flock; for it is your Father's good pleasure to give you the kingdom.   LUKE 12:32

For you have not received the spirit of bondage again to fear; but you have received the Spirit of adoption, whereby we cry, Abba, Father.   ROMANS 8:15

Nay, in all these things we are more than conquerors through Him that loved us. For I am persuaded, that neither death, nor life, nor angels, nor principalities, nor powers, nor things present, nor things to come, nor height, nor depth, nor any other creature, shall be able to separate us from the love of God, which is in Christ Jesus our Lord.   ROMANS 8:37–39

FRUSTRATION

Have not I commanded you? Be strong and of a good courage; be not afraid, neither be you dismayed: for the LORD *your God is with you wherever you go.* JOSHUA 1:9

Though I walk in the midst of trouble, You will revive me: You shall stretch forth Your hand against the wrath of my enemies, and Your right hand shall save me. The LORD *will perfect that which concerns me: Your mercy, O* LORD, *endures for ever: forsake not the works of Your own hands.* PSALM 138:7–8

In all your ways acknowledge Him, and He shall direct your paths. PROVERBS 3:6

Then shall we know, if we follow on to know the LORD: *His going forth is prepared as the morning; and He shall come unto us as the rain, as the latter and former rain to the earth.* HOSEA 6:3

Come to Me, all you that labor and are heavy laden, and I will give you rest. Take My yoke upon you, and learn of Me; for I am meek and lowly in heart: and you shall find rest to your souls. MATTHEW 11:28–29

What shall we then say to these things? If God be for us, who can be against us? He that spared not His own Son, but delivered Him up for us all, how shall He not with Him also freely give us all things? ROMANS 8:31–32

And let us not be weary in well doing: for in due season we shall reap, if we faint not. GALATIANS 6:9

Wherefore seeing we also are compassed about with so great a cloud of witnesses, let us lay aside every weight, and the sin which does so easily beset us, and let us run with patience the race that is set before us, looking to Jesus the author and finisher of our faith; who for the joy that was set before Him endured the cross, despising the shame, and is set down at the right hand of the throne of God. HEBREWS 12:1–2

My brethren, count it all joy when you fall into divers temptations; knowing this, that the trying of your faith works patience. But let patience have her perfect work, that you may be perfect and entire, wanting nothing. JAMES 1:2–4

INSIGHTS ON FAITH FROM SMITH WIGGLESWORTH

God is here now in power, in blessing, in might, and saying to you, my brother, and to you, my sister, "What is it? What is your request? Oh, He is so precious; He never fails; He is so wonderful! He always touches the needy place. He is so gentle; He never breaks the bruised reed. He is so rich in His mighty benevolence that He makes the smoking flax to flame.

〜

When you have a perfect confidence between you and God, it is amazing how your prayers rise, you catch fire, you are filled with zeal, your inspiration is tremendous, and you find out that the Spirit prays through you and that you live in a place of blessing.

〜

Brothers and sisters, what do you want? That is the question. What have you come here for? We have seen God work in horribly diseased bodies. Our God is able to heal and to meet all of our needs. The Scripture says: *"He who did not spare His own Son, but delivered Him up for us all, how shall He not with Him also freely give us all things?"* (Romans 8:32).

LONELINESS

And, behold, I am with you, and will keep you in all places wherever you go, and will bring you again into this land; for I will not leave you, until I have done that which I have spoken to you of.

GENESIS 28:15

When my father and my mother forsake me, then the LORD will take me up. PSALM 27:10

Lord, all my desire is before You; and my groaning is not hid from You. PSALM 38:9

But I am poor and needy; yet the Lord thinks upon me: You are my help and my deliverer; make no tarrying, O my God.

PSALM 40:17

Trust in Him at all times; you people, pour out your heart before him: God is a refuge for us. PSALM 62:8

A father of the fatherless, and a judge of the widows, is God in His holy habitation. God sets the solitary in families: He brings out those which are bound with chains: but the rebellious dwell in a dry land. PSALM 68:5–6

I will lift up my eyes to the hills, from where comes my help. My help comes from the LORD, which made heaven and earth.

SMALLCAPS

PSALM 121:1–2

Fear you not; for I am with you: be not dismayed; for I am Your God: I will strengthen you; yea, I will help you; yea, I will uphold you with the right hand of My righteousness.   ISAIAH 41:10

I will not leave you comfortless: I will come to you.   JOHN 14:18

Let your conversation be without covetousness; and be content with such things as you have: for He has said, I will never leave you, nor forsake you.   HEBREWS 13:5

Lo, I am with you always, even to the end of the world.

MATTHEW 28:20

OPPRESSION

The LORD also will be a refuge for the oppressed, a refuge in times of trouble.   PSALM 9:9

The LORD is near to them that are of a broken heart; and saves such as be of a contrite spirit.   PSALM 34:18

Yet sets He the poor on high from affliction, and makes him families like a flock. The righteous shall see it, and rejoice: and all iniquity shall stop her mouth. Whoso is wise, and will observe these things, even they shall understand the lovingkindness of the LORD.   PSALM 107:41–43

Deliver me from the oppression of man: so will I keep Your precepts.   PSALM 119:134

He that oppresses the poor reproaches his Maker: but he that honors Him has mercy on the poor.   PROVERBS 14:31

Learn to do well; seek judgment, relieve the oppressed, judge the fatherless, plead for the widow.   ISAIAH 1:17

INSIGHTS ON FAITH FROM SMITH WIGGLESWORTH

When you have a perfect confidence between you and God, it is amazing how your prayers rise. You catch fire, you are filled with zeal, your inspiration is tremendous, you find out that the Spirit prays through you, and you live in a place of blessing.

⌒

People say, "Could anything be greater than the fellowship that prevailed in the Garden of Eden when God walked and talked and had fellowship with man?" Yes, redemption is greater. Redemption is, therefore, greater than the garden of Eden, and God wants you to know that you may receive this glorious redemption not only for salvation, but also for the restoration of your bodies.

⌒

God has a choice for us all so that we might lose ourselves in God in a way we have never done before. I want to provoke you to love so that you will come into a place of blessing, for God wants you to be blessed so that you will be a blessing.

OPPRESSION

In righteousness shall you be established: you shall be far from oppression; for you shall not fear: and from terror; for it shall not come near you.   ISAIAH 54:14

But the Comforter, which is the Holy Ghost, whom the Father will send in My name, He shall teach you all things, and bring all things to your remembrance, whatsoever I have said to you.
                                                          JOHN 14:26

For he is the minister of God to you for good. But if you do that which is evil, be afraid; for he bears not the sword in vain: for he is the minister of God, a revenger to execute wrath upon him that does evil.   ROMANS 13:4

Put on the whole armor of God, that you may be able to stand against the wiles of the devil. For we wrestle not against flesh and blood, but against principalities, against powers, against the rulers of the darkness of this world, against spiritual wickedness in high places.   EPHESIANS 6:11–12

Above all, taking the shield of faith, wherewith you shall be able to quench all the fiery darts of the wicked.   EPHESIANS 6:16

For whatsoever is born of God overcomes the world: and this is the victory that overcomes the world, even our faith. 1 JOHN 5:4

PERSEVERANCE

Many are the afflictions of the righteous: but the LORD delivers him out of them all. PSALM 34:19

Though he fall, he shall not be utterly cast down: for the LORD upholds him with His hand. PSALM 37:24

And call upon Me in the day of trouble: I will deliver you, and you shall glorify Me. PSALM 50:15

Before I was afflicted I went astray: but now have I kept Your word. PSALM 119:67

Though I walk in the midst of trouble, You will revive me: You shall stretch forth Your hand against the wrath of my enemies, and Your right hand shall save me. PSALM 138:7

When you pass through the waters, I will be with you; and through the rivers, they shall not overflow you: when you walk through the fire, you shall not be burned; neither shall the flame kindle upon you. ISAIAH 43:2

Behold, I have refined you, but not with silver; I have chosen you in the furnace of affliction. ISAIAH 48:10

In your patience possess you your souls.   LUKE 21:19

For our light affliction, which is but for a moment, works for us a far more exceeding and eternal weight of glory.

2 CORINTHIANS 4:17

And not only so, but we glory in tribulations also: knowing that tribulation works patience; and patience, experience; and experience, hope: and hope makes not ashamed; because the love of God is shed abroad in our hearts by the Holy Ghost which is given to us.   ROMANS 5:3–5

For I reckon that the sufferings of this present time are not worthy to be compared with the glory which shall be revealed in us.

ROMANS 8:18

And we know that all things work together for good to them that love God, to them who are the called according to His purpose.

ROMANS 8:28

INSIGHTS ON FAITH FROM SMITH WIGGLESWORTH

What would happen if we learned the secret to asking once and then believing? What an advantage it would be if we could come to a place where we know that everything is within reach of us. God wants us to see that every obstacle can be removed. God brings us into a place where the difficulties are, where the pressure is, where the hard corner is, where everything is so difficult that you know there are no possibilities on the human side. God must do it.

God allows trials, difficulties, temptations, and perplexities to come right along our path, but there is not a temptation or trial that can come to us without God providing a way out. (See 1 Corinthians 10:13.)

Give God your life, and you will see that sickness has to go when God comes in fully. Then you are to walk before God, and you will find that He will perfect what concerns you. That is the place where He wants believers to live, the place where the Spirit of the Lord comes into your whole being. That is the place of victory.

SELF-IMAGE

I will praise You; for I am fearfully and wonderfully made: marvellous are Your works; and that my soul knows right well.

PSALM 139:14

He has made every thing beautiful in its time: also He has set the world in their heart, so that no man can find out the work that God makes from the beginning to the end. I know that there is no good in them, but for a man to rejoice, and to do good in his life.

ECCLESIASTES 3:11–12

For I know the thoughts that I think toward you, says the LORD, thoughts of peace, and not of evil, to give you an expected end.

JEREMIAH 29:11

I am the vine, you are the branches: He that abides in Me, and I in him, the same brings forth much fruit: for without Me you can do nothing.

JOHN 15:5

I beseech you therefore, brethren, by the mercies of God, that you present your bodies a living sacrifice, holy, acceptable to God, which is your reasonable service. And be not conformed to this world: but be you transformed by the renewing of your mind, that you may prove what is that good, and acceptable, and perfect, will of God.

ROMANS 12:1–2

STRESS

He makes me to lie down in green pastures: He leads me beside the still waters. He restores my soul: He leads me in the paths of righteousness for His name's sake.   PSALM 23:2–3

Heaviness in the heart of man makes it stoop: but a good word makes it glad.   PROVERBS 12:25

For thus says the Lord GOD, the Holy One of Israel; In returning and rest shall you be saved; in quietness and in confidence shall be your strength.   ISAIAH 30:15

The LORD God is my strength, and He will make my feet like hinds' feet, and He will make me to walk upon my high places.   HABAKKUK 3:19

Come to Me, all you that labor and are heavy laden, and I will give you rest. Take My yoke upon you, and learn of Me; for I am meek and lowly in heart: and you shall find rest to your souls. For My yoke is easy, and My burden is light. MATTHEW 11:28–30

Be careful for nothing; but in every thing by prayer and supplication with thanksgiving let your requests be made known to God.   PHILIPPIANS 4:6

TROUBLE

The LORD is my rock, and my fortress, and my deliverer; my God, my strength, in whom I will trust; my buckler, and the horn of my salvation, and my high tower. I will call upon the LORD, who is worthy to be praised: so shall I be saved from my enemies.

PSALM 18:2–3

For in the time of trouble He shall hide me in His pavilion: in the secret of His tabernacle shall He hide me; He shall set me up upon a rock.

PSALM 27:5

I will be glad and rejoice in Your mercy: for You have considered my trouble; You have known my soul in adversities; and have not shut me up into the hand of the enemy: You have set my feet in a large room. Have mercy upon me, O LORD, for I am in trouble: my eye is consumed with grief, yea, my soul and my belly.

PSALM 31:7–9

God is our refuge and strength, a very present help in trouble.

PSALM 46:1

Cast your burden upon the LORD, and He shall sustain you: He shall never allow the righteous to be moved.   PSALM 55:22

INSIGHTS ON FAITH FROM SMITH WIGGLESWORTH

Never be afraid of anything. There are two things in the world: one is fear, the other faith. One belongs to the Devil; the other to God. If you believe in God, there is no fear. If you sway toward any delusion of Satan, you will be brought into fear. Fear always brings bondage. There is a place of perfect love for Christ in which you are always casting out all fear and you are living in the place of freedom. (See 1 John 4:18.) Be sure that you never allow anything to make you afraid. God is for you; who can be against you?

God is with us in all circumstances, afflictions, persecutions; in every one of our trials, He is girding us with truth.

God has ten thousand more thoughts for you than you have for yourself. The grace of God is going to move us on, and you will never sorrow anymore as long as you live. You will never weep anymore, but you will weep for joy.

"BELIEVE THAT HE IS IN YOU. BELIEVE THAT HE IS ALMIGHTINESS. BELIEVE THAT HE IS ALL FULLNESS. THEN LET YOURSELF GO UNTIL HE IS ON THE THRONE OF YOUR HEART. LET EVERYTHING SUBMIT ITSELF TO GOD'S THRONE AND THE KING. YIELD YOURSELF UNTO HIM IN SO SUBLIME A POSITION THAT HE IS IN PERFECT ORDER OVER EVERYTHING."

—SMITH WIGGLESWORTH

3

FAITH THAT DELIVERS

ACTIVATING YOUR FAITH

I create the fruit of the lips; Peace, peace to him that is far off, and to him that is near, says the LORD; and I will heal him.

ISAIAH 57:19

When she had heard of Jesus, came in the press behind, and touched His garment. For she said, If I may touch but His clothes, I shall be whole. MARK 5:27–28

And the apostles said to the Lord, Increase our faith. And the Lord said, If you had faith as a grain of mustard seed, you might say to this sycamine tree, Be you plucked up by the root, and be you planted in the sea; and it should obey you. LUKE 17:5–6

Even so faith, if it has not works, is dead, being alone. JAMES 2:17

Being born again, not of corruptible seed, but of incorruptible, by the word of God, which lives and abides for ever. 1 PETER 1:23

ASSURANCE

And God is able to make all grace abound toward you; that you, always having all sufficiency in all things, may abound to every good work.   2 CORINTHIANS 9:8

According to the eternal purpose which He purposed in Christ Jesus our Lord: in whom we have boldness and access with confidence by the faith of Him.   EPHESIANS 3:11–12

For the which cause I also suffer these things: nevertheless I am not ashamed: for I know whom I have believed, and am persuaded that He is able to keep that which I have committed to him against that day.   2 TIMOTHY 1:12

And hereby we know that we are of the truth, and shall assure our hearts before Him. For if our heart condemn us, God is greater than our heart, and knows all things. Beloved, if our heart condemn us not, then have we confidence toward God.

1 JOHN 3:19–21

These things have I written to you that believe on the name of the Son of God; that you may know that you have eternal life, and that you may believe on the name of the Son of God.

1 JOHN 5:13

AUTHORITY

My mouth shall speak of wisdom; and the meditation of my heart shall be of understanding.　　　　　　　　Psalm 49:3

My son, let not them depart from your eyes: keep sound wisdom and discretion: So shall they be life to your soul, and grace to your neck. Then shall you walk in your way safely, and your foot shall not stumble.　　　　　　　　Proverbs 3:21–23

However when He, the Spirit of truth, is come, He will guide you into all truth: for He shall not speak of Himself; but whatsoever He shall hear, that shall He speak: and He will show you things to come.　　　　　　　　John 16:13

And He said to me, My grace is sufficient for you: for My strength is made perfect in weakness. Most gladly therefore will I rather glory in my infirmities, that the power of Christ may rest upon me.　　　　　　　　2 Corinthians 12:9

That He would grant you, according to the riches of His glory, to be strengthened with might by His Spirit in the inner man; that Christ may dwell in your hearts by faith; that you, being rooted and grounded in love, may be able to comprehend with all saints what is the breadth, and length, and depth, and height.

Ephesians 3:16–18

INSIGHTS ON FAITH FROM SMITH WIGGLESWORTH

Faith is a mighty power. Faith will reach at everything. When real faith comes into operation, you will not say, "I don't feel much better." Faith says, "I am whole." Faith doesn't say, "I have a lame leg." Faith says, "My leg is all right."

~

We should be awake to the fact that we must believe; we must know the Scriptures and rest unconditionally, absolutely, upon the Word of God. God has never failed anyone who relied on His Word. Some human plan or your mind may come between you and God's Word, but rest upon what God's Word says. "Only believe." Oh, the charm of that truth, making you rich forever, taking away all weariness.

~

Have faith in God! If I believe, then what? I receive what I wish, as I begin to speak. God brings it to pass—not just with a fig tree, but even with a mountain (see Matthew 21:19–22)—whatever you say.

BELIEF

Jesus said to him, If you can believe, all things are possible to him that believes.   MARK 9:23

But as many as received Him, to them gave He power to become the sons of God, even to them that believe on His name.
                                                                JOHN 1:12

And Jesus said to them, I am the bread of life: he that comes to Me shall never hunger; and he that believes on Me shall never thirst.
                                                                JOHN 6:35

I am come a light into the world, that whosoever believes on Me should not abide in darkness.   JOHN 12:46

And they said, Believe on the Lord Jesus Christ, and you shall be saved, and your house.   ACTS 16:31

Wherefore also it is contained in the scripture, Behold, I lay in Zion a chief corner stone, elect, precious: and he that believes on Him shall not be confounded.   1 PETER 2:6

BINDING THE ENEMY SPIRIT

Your right hand, O LORD, is become glorious in power: Your right hand, O LORD, has dashed in pieces the enemy. And in the greatness of Your excellency You have overthrown them that rose up against You: You sent forth Your wrath, which consumed them as stubble. EXODUS 15:6–7

None is so fierce that dare stir him up: who then is able to stand before Me? JOB 41:10

The LORD on high is mightier than the noise of many waters, yea, than the mighty waves of the sea. PSALM 93:4

Then they cry to the LORD in their trouble, and he brings them out of their distresses. He makes the storm a calm, so that the waves thereof are still. PSALM 107:28–29

In that day the LORD with His sore and great and strong sword shall punish leviathan the piercing serpent, even leviathan that crooked serpent; and He shall slay the dragon that is in the sea. ISAIAH 27:1

Thus says the LORD, which makes a way in the sea, and a path in the mighty waters. ISAIAH 43:16

And I will give to you the keys of the kingdom of heaven: and whatsoever you shall bind on earth shall be bound in heaven: and whatsoever you shall loose on earth shall be loosed in heaven.

MATTHEW 16:19

Verily I say to you, Whatsoever you shall bind on earth shall be bound in heaven: and whatsoever you shall loose on earth shall be loosed in heaven.

MATTHEW 18:18

To open their eyes, and to turn them from darkness to light, and from the power of Satan to God, that they may receive forgiveness of sins, and inheritance among them which are sanctified by faith that is in Me.

ACTS 26:18

Behold, I give to you power to tread on serpents and scorpions, and over all the power of the enemy: and nothing shall by any means hurt you.

LUKE 10:19

Beloved, believe not every spirit, but try the spirits whether they are of God: because many false prophets are gone out into the world.

1 JOHN 4:1

INSIGHTS ON FAITH FROM SMITH WIGGLESWORTH

What are you ready for now? Are you ready for anything? Don't forget you have to go over the top. The top of what? The top of yourself, the top of your opinions and fancies and whims and foolish acts. You have to dethrone them; you have to have a biblical building; you have to be in the Scriptures. *"For God has not given us a spirit of fear, but of power and of love and of a sound mind"* (2 Timothy 1:7).

There is a rest of faith if we have entered into it, if we have *"ceased from* [our] *own works"* (Hebrews 4:10), ceased from our own struggling, ceased from making our own plans. It is a rest in faith, a place where you can smile in the face of any disruption. No matter what comes, you will be in the place of real rest.

I tell you, my dear ones, it is impossible for God to fail you. I tell you, my dear ones, it is impossible for God to fail you. If you hear the Word of God, it will so stimulate you that you will know as sure as you live that God will bring you out of your condition.

BLESSINGS

And Jabez called on the God of Israel, saying, Oh that You would bless me indeed, and enlarge my coast, and that Your hand might be with me, and that You would keep me from evil, that it may not grieve me! And God granted him that which he requested.

1 CHRONICLES 4:10

I have called upon You, for You will hear me, O God: incline Your ear to me, and hear my speech. Show Your marvellous lovingkindness, O You that save by Your right hand them which put their trust in You from those that rise up against them. Keep me as the apple of the eye, hide me under the shadow of Your wings, from the wicked that oppress me, from my deadly enemies, who compass me about.

PSALM 17:6–9

I will sing of the mercies of the LORD for ever: with my mouth will I make known Your faithfulness to all generations. For I have said, Mercy shall be built up for ever: Your faithfulness shall You establish in the very heavens.

PSALMS 89:1–2

The LORD has been mindful of us: He will bless us; He will bless the house of Israel; He will bless the house of Aaron. He will bless them that fear the LORD, both small and great. The LORD shall increase you more and more, you and your children.

PSALM 115:12–14

He that walks righteously, and speaks uprightly; he that despises the gain of oppressions, that shakes his hands from holding of bribes, that stops his ears from hearing of blood, and shuts his eyes from seeing evil; he shall dwell on high: his place of defence shall be the munitions of rocks: bread shall be given him; his waters shall be sure.   ISAIAH 33:15–16

For I the LORD your God will hold your right hand, saying to you, Fear not; I will help you.   ISAIAH 41:13

Follow peace with all men, and holiness, without which no man shall see the Lord.   HEBREWS 12:14

But the wisdom that is from above is first pure, then peaceable, gentle, and easy to be entreated, full of mercy and good fruits, without partiality, and without hypocrisy.   JAMES 3:17

For he that will love life, and see good days, let him refrain his tongue from evil, and his lips that they speak no guile: let him eschew evil, and do good; let him seek peace, and ensue it.
                                                    1 PETER 3:10–11

BREAKTHROUGH

Surely He shall deliver you from the snare of the fowler, and from the noisome pestilence. He shall cover you with His feathers, and under His wings shall you trust: His truth shall be your shield and buckler. You shall not be afraid for the terror by night; nor for the arrow that flies by day.　　　　　PSALM 91:3–5

No weapon that is formed against you shall prosper; and every tongue that shall rise against you in judgment you shall condemn. This is the heritage of the servants of the LORD, and their righteousness is of Me, says the LORD.　　　　　ISAIAH 54:17

Call to Me, and I will answer you, and show you great and mighty things, which you know not.　　　　　JEREMIAH 33:3

It is of the LORD's mercies that we are not consumed, because His compassions fail not. They are new every morning: great is Your faithfulness.　　　　　LAMENTATIONS 3:22–23

You are of God, little children, and have overcome them: because greater is He that is in you, than he that is in the world.

1 JOHN 4:4

INSIGHTS ON FAITH FROM SMITH WIGGLESWORTH

What I want to impress upon you is that we must see these greater works that the Lord promised we would see. Let us hear the words of our Lord again: *"Greater works than these* [you] *will do, because I go to My Father. And whatever you ask in My name, that I will do, that the Father may be glorified in the Son"* (John 14:12–13). What is it that you want? *"Whatever you ask in My name, that I will do."* Glory to God. Is there any purpose in it? Yes, *"that the Father may be glorified in the Son."*

⁓

Beloved, believe today that God has a way for you. Perhaps you have never come that way before. God has a way beyond all your ways of thought. He has a choice and a plan for you.

⁓

My brother, my sister, you have been nearly weighed down with troubles. They have almost crushed you. Sometimes you thought you would never get out of this place of difficulty, but you have no idea that behind the whole thing, God has been working a plan greater than all.

CHANGE

Be strong and of a good courage, fear not, nor be afraid of them: for the LORD your God, He it is that does go with you; He will not fail you, nor forsake you. DEUTERONOMY 31:6

The eternal God is your refuge, and underneath are the everlasting arms: and He shall thrust out the enemy from before you; and shall say, Destroy them. DEUTERONOMY 33:27

There shall not any man be able to stand before you all the days of your life: as I was with Moses, so I will be with you: I will not fail you, nor forsake you. JOSHUA 1:5

Have not I commanded you? Be strong and of a good courage; be not afraid, neither be you dismayed: for the LORD your God is with you wherever you go. JOSHUA 1:9

He asked life of You, and You gave it him, even length of days for ever and ever. PSALM 21:4

They shall still bring forth fruit in old age; they shall be fat and flourishing; to show that the LORD is upright: He is my rock, and there is no unrighteousness in Him. PSALM 92:14–15

The fear of the LORD prolongs days: but the years of the wicked shall be shortened. PROVERBS 10:27

For I am the LORD, I change not; therefore you sons of Jacob are not consumed. MALACHI 3:6

I beseech you therefore, brethren, by the mercies of God, that you present your bodies a living sacrifice, holy, acceptable to God, which is your reasonable service. And be not conformed to this world: but be you transformed by the renewing of your mind, that you may prove what is that good, and acceptable, and perfect, will of God. ROMANS 12:1–2

Not by works of righteousness which we have done, but according to His mercy He saved us, by the washing of regeneration, and renewing of the Holy Ghost. TITUS 3:5

EMOTIONAL NEEDS

For he shall deliver the needy when he cries; the poor also, and him that has no helper. PSALM 72:12

When you go, your steps shall not be straitened; and when you run, you shall not stumble. Take fast hold of instruction; let her not go: keep her; for she is your life. PROVERBS 4:12–13

God is faithful, by whom you were called to the fellowship of His Son Jesus Christ our Lord. 1 CORINTHIANS 1:9

Now our Lord Jesus Christ himself, and God, even our Father, which has loved us, and has given us everlasting consolation and good hope through grace, comfort your hearts, and establish you in every good word and work. 2 THESSALONIANS 2:16–17

For God has not given us the spirit of fear; but of power, and of love, and of a sound mind. 2 TIMOTHY 1:7

For you have not received the spirit of bondage again to fear; but you have received the Spirit of adoption, whereby we cry, Abba, Father. ROMANS 8:15–16

INSIGHTS ON FAITH FROM SMITH WIGGLESWORTH

It is in the furnace of affliction that God gets us to the place where He can use us. Paul said concerning difficulty, "I do and will rejoice." (See Philippians 1:18.) *"For I know that this will turn out for my deliverance through your prayer and the supply of the Spirit of Jesus Christ…[that] Christ will be magnified in my body"* (verse 19). Before God puts you in the furnace, He knows that you will make it through it. He never gives us anything that is above what we are able to bear.

⌣

If you know that it is scriptural to be healed of every weakness—to be holy and pure, to overcome in the midst of all conditions—never rest until you are an overcomer.

⌣

The Lord may permit your tire to be punctured many times, but you must not be discouraged that the air has gone out. You must pump it up again. The life that He began cannot be taken away from you. If you have an inspiration to "go forth," you cannot be stopped. You know you are called to an eternal purpose, and nothing will stand in your way. It is His purpose that we will be sanctified, purified, and renewed.

FAITHFULNESS OF GOD

And the LORD passed by before him, and proclaimed, The LORD, The LORD God, merciful and gracious, longsuffering, and abundant in goodness and truth. EXODUS 34:6

God is not a man, that He should lie; neither the son of man, that He should repent: has He said, and shall He not do it? or has He spoken, and shall He not make it good? NUMBERS 23:19

Know therefore that the LORD your God, He is God, the faithful God, which keeps covenant and mercy with them that love Him and keep His commandments to a thousand generations. DEUTERONOMY 7:9

He shall send from heaven, and save me from the reproach of him that would swallow me up. God shall send forth His mercy and His truth. PSALM 57:3

My covenant will I not break, nor alter the thing that is gone out of My lips. PSALM 89:34

He shall cover you with His feathers, and under His wings shall you trust: His truth shall be your shield and buckler. PSALM 91:4

For the LORD is good; His mercy is everlasting; and His truth endures to all generations. PSALM 100:5

For ever, O Lord, Your word is settled in heaven. Your faithfulness is to all generations: You have established the earth, and it abides.   Psalm 119:89–90

Your word is true from the beginning: and every one of Your righteous judgments endures for ever.   Psalm 119:160

Let not mercy and truth forsake you: bind them about your neck; write them upon the table of your heart: so shall you find favor and good understanding in the sight of God and man.

Proverbs 3:3–4

This I recall to my mind, therefore have I hope. It is of the Lord's mercies that we are not consumed, because His compassions fail not. They are new every morning: great is Your faithfulness.

Lamentations 3:21–23

Then touched He their eyes, saying, According to your faith be it to you.   Matthew 9:29

And Jesus answering says to them, Have faith in God. For verily I say to you, That whosoever shall say to this mountain, Be you removed, and be you cast into the sea; and shall not doubt in his heart, but shall believe that those things which he says shall come to pass; he shall have whatsoever he says.   Mark 11:22–23

INSIGHTS ON FAITH FROM SMITH WIGGLESWORTH

Thank God, if we believe, all things are possible. (See Mark 9:23.) It can be done now, this moment as you sit in your seat, if you believe it will be done for the glory of God. Now I want a wholesale healing today. I believe it may be possible for some to have that divine, inward moving of living faith that will make them absolutely whole. If you will deny yourself and believe God's Word, you will be healed at the touch of the Lord. Now I want you to live in the sunshine.

Yes, there is a power, a blessing, an assurance, a rest in the presence of the Holy Spirit. You can feel His presence and know that He is with you. You do not need to spend an hour without this inner knowledge of His holy presence. With His power upon you, there can be no failure.

FAITHFULNESS OF GOD

For therein is the righteousness of God revealed from faith to faith: as it is written, The just shall live by faith.   ROMANS 1:17

For all the promises of God in Him are yea, and in Him Amen, to the glory of God by us.   2 CORINTHIANS 1:20

For we walk by faith, not by sight.   2 CORINTHIANS 5:7

For by grace are you saved through faith; and that not of yourselves: it is the gift of God.   EPHESIANS 2:8

As you have therefore received Christ Jesus the Lord, so walk you in Him: rooted and built up in Him, and stablished in the faith, as you have been taught, abounding therein with thanksgiving.
   COLOSSIANS 2:6–7

But continue you in the things which you have learned and have been assured of, knowing of whom you have learned them; and that from a child you have known the holy scriptures, which are able to make you wise to salvation through faith which is in Christ Jesus.   2 TIMOTHY 3:14–15

FAVOR OF GOD

God be merciful to us, and bless us; and cause His face to shine upon us. ...God shall bless us; and all the ends of the earth shall fear Him.   PSALM 67:1, 7

Remember me, O LORD, with the favor that You bear to Your people: O visit me with Your salvation.   PSALM 106:4

No weapon that is formed against you shall prosper; and every tongue that shall rise against you in judgment you shall condemn. This is the heritage of the servants of the LORD, and their righteousness is of Me, says the LORD.   ISAIAH 54:17

To proclaim the acceptable year of the LORD, and the day of vengeance of our God; to comfort all that mourn.   ISAIAH 61:2

And I will restore to you the years that the locust has eaten, the cankerworm, and the caterpillar, and the palmerworm, My great army which I sent among you.   JOEL 2:25

And the Child grew, and waxed strong in spirit, filled with wisdom: and the grace of God was upon Him.   LUKE 2:40

For the weapons of our warfare are not carnal, but mighty through God to the pulling down of strong holds.   2 CORINTHIANS 10:4

INSIGHTS ON FAITH FROM SMITH WIGGLESWORTH

When they were outside, one of the six said, "There is one thing we could have done. I wish you would all go back with me and try it." They all went back and got together in a group. This brother said, "Let us whisper the name of Jesus." At first, when they whispered this worthy name, nothing seemed to happen. But as they continued to whisper "Jesus! Jesus! Jesus!" the power began to fall. As they saw that God was beginning to work, their faith and joy increased, and they whispered the name louder and louder. As they did so, the man rose from his bed and dressed himself. The secret was just this: those six people had gotten their eyes off the sick man and were taken up with the Lord Jesus Himself. Their faith grasped the power in His name. Oh, if people would only appreciate the power in this name, there is no telling what would happen.

It is a blessed thing to learn that God's Word can never fail. Never listen to human plans. God can work mightily when you persist in believing Him in spite of discouragement from the human standpoint.

GOD'S CARE

But You, O Lord, are a shield for me; my glory, and the lifter up of my head. PSALM 3:3

The Lord is my shepherd; I shall not want. He makes me to lie down in green pastures: He leads me beside the still waters. He restores my soul: He leads me in the paths of righteousness for His name's sake. PSALM 23:1–3

For it was not an enemy that reproached me; then I could have borne it: neither was it he that hated me that did magnify himself against me; then I would have hid myself from him. PSALM 55:12

Blessed be the Lord, who daily loads us with benefits, even the God of our salvation. PSALM 68:19

I love the Lord, because He has heard my voice and my supplications. PSALM 116:1

I will abundantly bless her provision: I will satisfy her poor with bread. PSALM 132:15

For You have possessed my reins: You have covered me in my mother's womb. PSALM 139:13

It is of the LORD's mercies that we are not consumed, because His compassions fail not. They are new every morning: great is Your faithfulness. The LORD is my portion, says my soul; therefore will I hope in Him. The LORD is good to them that wait for Him, to the soul that seeks Him. It is good that a man should both hope and quietly wait for the salvation of the LORD.

LAMENTATIONS 3:22–26

But this thing commanded I them, saying, Obey My voice, and I will be your God, and you shall be My people: and walk you in all the ways that I have commanded you, that it may be well to you.

JEREMIAH 7:23

Are not two sparrows sold for a farthing? and one of them shall not fall on the ground without your Father. But the very hairs of your head are all numbered. Fear you not therefore, you are of more value than many sparrows. MATTHEW 10:29–31

He that spared not His own Son, but delivered Him up for us all, how shall He not with Him also freely give us all things?

ROMANS 8:32

Not that we are sufficient of ourselves to think any thing as of ourselves; but our sufficiency is of God. 2 CORINTHIANS 3:5

Not that I speak in respect of want: for I have learned, in whatsoever state I am, therewith to be content. I know both how to be abased, and I know how to abound: every where and in all things I am instructed both to be full and to be hungry, both to abound and to suffer need.   PHILIPPIANS 4:11–12

I can do all things through Christ which strengthens me.
                    PHILIPPIANS 4:13

You are of God, little children, and have overcome them: because greater is He that is in you, than he that is in the world.
                    1 JOHN 4:4

And God shall wipe away all tears from their eyes; and there shall be no more death, neither sorrow, nor crying, neither shall there be any more pain: for the former things are passed away.
                    REVELATION 21:4

Casting all your care upon Him; for He cares for you.
                    1 PETER 5:7

INSIGHTS ON FAITH FROM SMITH WIGGLESWORTH

Where faith is undisturbed, there is peace. I am speaking of eternal faith, daring to believe what God has said. If I dare to trust Him, I find that what He has said always comes to pass. We must not doubt. *"He who doubts is like a wave of the sea driven and tossed by the wind. For let not that man suppose that he will receive anything from the Lord"* (James 1:6–7). Have faith in God.

⌒

Know the wisdom and purpose of God's great hand upon you. Glorify God in distresses and persecution, for the Spirit of God is made manifest in these situations. Be chastened! Be perfected! Press on to heights, depths, breadths. Faith is the victory. (See 1 John 5:4.) The hope is within you. (See 1 Peter 3:15.) The joy is set before you. (See Hebrews 12:2.) God gives the peace that passes all understanding. (See Philippians 4:7.) We know that the flesh has withered in the presence of the purifying of the Word. He who has brought you to this point will take you to the end.

"DO YOU THINK THAT GOD MADE YOU IN ORDER TO WATCH YOU FAIL? GOD NEVER MADE MEN IN ORDER TO SEE THEM FAIL. HE MADE MEN IN ORDER THAT THEY MIGHT BE SONS WHO WALK THE EARTH IN POWER. SO WHEN I LOOK AT YOU, I KNOW THAT GOD CAN GIVE YOU THE CAPABILITY TO BRING EVERYTHING INTO SUBJECTION."

—SMITH WIGGLESWORTH

4

WORDS OF LIFE

GRACE

For if you turn again to the LORD, your brethren and your children shall find compassion before them that lead them captive, so that they shall come again into this land: for the LORD your God is gracious and merciful, and will not turn away His face from you, if you return to Him.   2 CHRONICLES 30:9

The righteous also shall hold on his way, and he that has clean hands shall be stronger and stronger.   JOB 17:9

The LORD will perfect that which concerns me: Your mercy, O LORD, endures for ever: forsake not the works of Your own hands.   PSALM 138:8

Let the wicked forsake his way, and the unrighteous man his thoughts: and let him return to the LORD, and He will have mercy upon him; and to our God, for He will abundantly pardon.

ISAIAH 55:7

And of His fullness have all we received, and grace for grace.

JOHN 1:16

Jesus says to him, Rise, take up your bed, and walk.   JOHN 5:8

And if by grace, then is it no more of works: otherwise grace is no more grace. But if it be of works, then it is no more grace: otherwise work is no more work.   ROMANS 11:6

But by the grace of God I am what I am: and His grace which was bestowed upon me was not in vain; but I labored more abundantly than they all: yet not I, but the grace of God which was with me.   1 CORINTHIANS 15:10

Therefore if any man be in Christ, he is a new creature: old things are passed away; behold, all things are become new.

2 CORINTHIANS 5:17

And God is able to make all grace abound toward you; that you, always having all sufficiency in all things, may abound to every good work.   2 CORINTHIANS 9:8

And He said to me, My grace is sufficient for you: for My strength is made perfect in weakness. Most gladly therefore will I rather glory in my infirmities, that the power of Christ may rest upon me.   2 CORINTHIANS 12:9

Which is come to you, as it is in all the world; and brings forth fruit, as it does also in you, since the day you heard of it, and knew the grace of God in truth.   COLOSSIANS 1:6

For by grace are you saved through faith; and that not of yourselves: it is the gift of God: Not of works, lest any man should boast.   EPHESIANS 2:8–9

You therefore, my son, be strong in the grace that is in Christ Jesus.   2 TIMOTHY 2:1

For we have not an high priest which cannot be touched with the feeling of our infirmities; but was in all points tempted like as we are, yet without sin. Let us therefore come boldly to the throne of grace, that we may obtain mercy, and find grace to help in time of need.   HEBREWS 4:15–16

But He gives more grace. Wherefore He says, God resists the proud, but gives grace to the humble.   JAMES 4:6

INSIGHTS ON FAITH FROM SMITH WIGGLESWORTH

We have a big God. We have a wonderful Jesus. We have a glorious Comforter. God's canopy is over you and will cover you at all times, preserving you from evil. *"Under His wings you shall take refuge"* (Psalm 91:4). *"The word of God is living and powerful"* (Hebrews 4:12), and in its treasures you will find eternal life. If you dare trust this wonderful Lord, this Lord of Life, you will find in Him everything you need.

⌒

The God who told Moses to make a bronze serpent and put it on a pole so that whoever looked could be healed (see Numbers 21:5–9), now says, "The bronze serpent is not on the pole. Jesus is not on the cross. He has risen and has been given all power and authority. Believe. You will be healed if you believe.

⌒

You cannot literally look at the cross, you cannot literally look at the serpent, but you can believe. If you believe, you can be healed. God means for you to believe today; God means for you to be helped today.

GUIDANCE

The LORD is my rock, and my fortress, and my deliverer; my God, my strength, in whom I will trust; my buckler, and the horn of my salvation, and my high tower.   PSALM 18:2

For You will light my candle: the LORD my God will enlighten my darkness.   PSALM 18:28

For He has not despised nor abhorred the affliction of the afflicted; neither has He hid His face from him; but when he cried to Him, He heard.   PSALM 22:24

The LORD is my strength and my shield; my heart trusted in Him, and I am helped: therefore my heart greatly rejoices; and with my song will I praise Him.   PSALM 28:7

For You are my rock and my fortress; therefore for Your name's sake lead me, and guide me.   PSALM 31:3

The steps of a good man are ordered by the LORD: and He delights in his way.   PSALM 37:23

For this God is our God for ever and ever: He will be our guide even to death.   PSALM 48:14

Nevertheless I am continually with You: You have held me by my right hand. You shall guide me with Your counsel, and afterward receive me to glory.   PSALM 73:23–24

My flesh and my heart fails: but God is the strength of my heart, and my portion for ever.   PSALM 73:26

Thy word is a lamp to my feet, and a light to my path.
PSALM 119:105

Trust in the LORD with all your heart; and lean not to your own understanding. In all your ways acknowledge Him, and He shall direct your paths.   PROVERBS 3:5–6

I have taught you in the way of wisdom; I have led you in right paths.   PROVERBS 4:11

Commit your works to the LORD, and your thoughts shall be established.   PROVERBS 16:3

Behold, the Lord GOD will help me; who is he that shall condemn me? lo, they all shall wax old as a garment; the moth shall eat them up.   ISAIAH 50:9

And the Lord *shall guide you continually, and satisfy your soul in drought, and make fat your bones: and you shall be like a watered garden, and like a spring of water, whose waters fail not.*

Isaiah 58:11

The Lord *is good, a strong hold in the day of trouble; and He knows them that trust in Him.* Nahum 1:7

But the Comforter, which is the Holy Ghost, whom the Father will send in My name, He shall teach you all things, and bring all things to your remembrance, whatsoever I have said to you.

John 14:26

If any of you lack wisdom, let him ask of God, that gives to all men liberally, and upbraids not; and it shall be given him. But let him ask in faith, nothing wavering. For he that wavers is like a wave of the sea driven with the wind and tossed. James 1:5–6

When He, the Spirit of truth, is come, He will guide you into all truth: for He shall not speak of Himself; but whatsoever He shall hear, that shall He speak: and He will show you things to come.

John 16:13

INSIGHTS ON FAITH FROM SMITH WIGGLESWORTH

I believe the Word of God is so powerful that it can transform any and every life. There is power in God's Word to make that which does not exist to appear. There is executive power in the words that proceed from His lips. The psalmist told us, *"He sent His word and healed them"* (Psalm 107:20). Do you think the Word has diminished in its power? I tell you, it has not. God's Word can bring things to pass today as it did in the past.

⌒

God wants you to have a living faith now; He wants you to get a vital touch, shaking the foundation of all weakness. When you were saved, you were saved the moment you believed, and you will be healed the moment you believe.

⌒

People miss the greatest plan of healing because of moving from one thing to another. Become stationary. God wants you to take the Word, claim the Word, and believe the Word. That is the perfect way of healing. Do not turn to the right hand or to the left (see Deuteronomy 5:32), but believe God.

HOPE

Be of good courage, and He shall strengthen your heart, all you that hope in the LORD. PSALM 31:24

For our heart shall rejoice in Him, because we have trusted in His holy name. Let Your mercy, O LORD, be upon us, according as we hope in You. PSALM 33:21–22

For in You, O LORD, do I hope: You will hear, O Lord my God. PSALM 38:15

Why are you cast down, O my soul? and why are you disquieted within me? hope you in God: for I shall yet praise Him, who is the health of my countenance, and my God. PSALM 42:11

For You are my hope, O Lord GOD: You are my trust from my youth. PSALM 71:5

But I will hope continually, and will yet praise You more and more. PSALM 71:14

Uphold me according to Your word, that I may live: and let me not be ashamed of my hope. PSALM 119:116

Blessed is the man that trusts in the LORD, and whose hope the LORD is. For he shall be as a tree planted by the waters, and that spreads out her roots by the river, and shall not see when heat comes, but her leaf shall be green; and shall not be careful in the year of drought, neither shall cease from yielding fruit.

JEREMIAH 17:7–8

The LORD is my portion, says my soul; therefore will I hope in him. The LORD is good to them that wait for Him, to the soul that seeks Him.

LAMENTATIONS 3:24–25

But they that wait upon the LORD shall renew their strength; they shall mount up with wings as eagles; they shall run, and not be weary; and they shall walk, and not faint.

ISAIAH 40:31

Therefore did my heart rejoice, and my tongue was glad; moreover also my flesh shall rest in hope: Because You will not leave my soul in hell, neither will You allow Your Holy One to see corruption. You have made known to me the ways of life; You shall make me full of joy with Your countenance.

ACTS 2:26–28

Rejoicing in hope; patient in tribulation; continuing instant in prayer.

ROMANS 12:12

Now the God of hope fill you with all joy and peace in believ-
ing, that you may abound in hope, through the power of the Holy
Ghost. ROMANS 15:13

Blessed be the God and Father of our Lord Jesus Christ, who
has blessed us with all spiritual blessings in heavenly places in
Christ. EPHESIANS 1:3

Now to Him that is able to do exceeding abundantly above all
that we ask or think, according to the power that works in us, to
Him be glory in the church by Christ Jesus throughout all ages,
world without end. Amen. EPHESIANS 3:20–21

Now faith is the substance of things hoped for, the evidence of
things not seen. HEBREWS 11:1

Blessed be the God and Father of our Lord Jesus Christ, which
according to His abundant mercy has begotten us again to a lively
hope by the resurrection of Jesus Christ from the dead.
1 PETER 1:3

Jesus said to him, If you can believe, all things are possible to him
that believes. MARK 9:23

INSIGHTS ON FAITH FROM SMITH WIGGLESWORTH

It is only He; it is He who rolls away the cloud. He alone is the One who lifts the fallen, cheers the faint, brings fresh oil, and changes the countenance. It is the Lord your God. He has seen your misery, He has known your brokenhearted-ness, and He has known how near you seem to be to despair. Oh, beloved, God is in the midst of us to help us into these wonderful divine places of appointment!

All our victories are won before we go into the fight. They are won as we pray. Prayer links us to our lovely God, our peaceful God, our abounding God, our multiplying God. Oh, I love Him. He is so wonderful!

LOVE

For Your lovingkindness is before my eyes: and I have walked in Your truth.   PSALM 26:3

Because he has set his love upon Me, therefore will I deliver him: I will set him on high, because he has known My name.
                                                                PSALM 91:14

For as the heaven is high above the earth, so great is His mercy toward them that fear Him. As far as the east is from the west, so far has He removed our transgressions from us.
                                                          PSALM 103:11–12

The LORD preserves all them that love Him: but all the wicked will He destroy.   PSALM 145:20

The LORD opens the eyes of the blind: the LORD raises them that are bowed down: the LORD loves the righteous.   PSALM 146:8

The LORD has appeared of old to me, saying, Yea, I have loved you with an everlasting love: therefore with lovingkindness have I drawn you.   JEREMIAH 31:3

It is of the LORD's mercies that we are not consumed, because His compassions fail not. They are new every morning: great is Your faithfulness.   LAMENTATIONS 3:22–23

The LORD your God in the midst of you is mighty; He will save, He will rejoice over you with joy; He will rest in His love, He will joy over you with singing.   ZEPHANIAH 3:17

Are not two sparrows sold for a farthing? and one of them shall not fall on the ground without your Father. But the very hairs of your head are all numbered. Fear you not therefore, you are of more value than many sparrows.   MATTHEW 10:29–31

And the glory which You gave Me I have given them; that they may be one, even as We are one: I in them, and You in Me, that they may be made perfect in one; and that the world may know that You have sent Me, and have loved them, as You have loved Me.   JOHN 17:22–23

But even the very hairs of your head are all numbered. Fear not therefore: you are of more value than many sparrows.

LUKE 12:7

Nay, in all these things we are more than conquerors through Him that loved us. For I am persuaded, that neither death, nor life, nor angels, nor principalities, nor powers, nor things present, nor things to come, nor height, nor depth, nor any other creature, shall be able to separate us from the love of God, which is in Christ Jesus our Lord.   ROMANS 8:37–39

But God, who is rich in mercy, for His great love wherewith He loved us, even when we were dead in sins, has quickened us together with Christ, by grace you are saved. And has raised us up together, and made us sit together in heavenly places in Christ Jesus: that in the ages to come He might show the exceeding riches of His grace in His kindness toward us through Christ Jesus.

EPHESIANS 2:4–7

He that loves not knows not God; for God is love.   1 JOHN 4:8

And we have known and believed the love that God has to us. God is love; and he that dwells in love dwells in God, and God in him.   1 JOHN 4:16

There is no fear in love; but perfect love casts out fear: because fear has torment. He that fears is not made perfect in love.

1 JOHN 4:18

INSIGHTS ON FAITH FROM SMITH WIGGLESWORTH

God has a million ways of undertaking for those who go to Him for help. He has deliverance for every captive. He loves you so much that He even says, *"Before they call, I will answer"* (Isaiah 65:24). Don't turn Him away.

⌒

You believe it is the Lord's will for you to suffer, but you are trying to get out of it as quickly as you can. You have medicine bottles all over the place. Get out of your hiding place, and confess that you are a sinner. If you'll get rid of your self-righteousness, God will do something for you. Drop the idea that you are so holy that God has to afflict you. Sin is the cause of your sickness, not righteousness. Disease is not caused by righteousness, but by sin.

⌒

"Come to Me, all you who labor and are heavy laden, and I will give you rest" (Matthew 11:28). God is willing in His great mercy to touch your limbs with His mighty power, and if He is willing to do this, how much more eager He is to deliver you from the power of Satan and to make you a child of the King! How much more necessary it is for you to be healed of your soul sickness than of your bodily ailments! And God is willing to give the double cure.

MERCY

And He said, I will make all My goodness pass before you, and I will proclaim the name of the LORD before you; and will be gracious to whom I will be gracious, and will show mercy on whom I will show mercy. EXODUS 33:19

For the LORD your God is a merciful God; He will not forsake You, neither destroy you, nor forget the covenant of your fathers which He swore to them. DEUTERONOMY 4:31

The LORD has heard my supplication; the LORD will receive my prayer. PSALM 6:9

Blessed be the LORD, because He has heard the voice of my supplications. PSALM 28:6

Your mercy, O LORD, is in the heavens; and you faithfulness reaches to the clouds. PSALM 36:5

Withhold not You Your tender mercies from me, O LORD: let Your lovingkindness and Your truth continually preserve me. PSALM 40:11

Have mercy upon me, O God, according to Your lovingkindness: according to the multitude of Your tender mercies blot out my transgressions. PSALM 51:1

Be merciful to me, O God, be merciful to me: for my soul trusts in You: yea, in the shadow of Your wings will I make my refuge, until these calamities be passed over.   PSALM 57:1

Hear me, O LORD; for Your lovingkindness is good: turn to me according to the multitude of Your tender mercies.

PSALM 69:16

You are the God that does wonders: You have declared Your strength among the people.   PSALM 77:14

But the mercy of the LORD is from everlasting to everlasting upon them that fear Him, and His righteousness to children's children.   PSALM 103:17

Hear my prayer, O LORD, give ear to my supplications: in Your faithfulness answer me, and in Your righteousness.

PSALM 143:1

For My name's sake will I defer My anger, and for My praise will I refrain for you, that I cut you not off.   ISAIAH 48:9

In all their affliction He was afflicted, and the angel of His presence saved them: in His love and in His pity He redeemed them; and He bare them, and carried them all the days of old.

ISAIAH 63:9

He has showed you, O man, what is good; and what does the LORD require of you, but to do justly, and to love mercy, and to walk humbly with your God?

MICAH 6:8

Blessed are the merciful: for they shall obtain mercy.

MATTHEW 5:7

And His mercy is on them that fear Him from generation to generation.

LUKE 1:50

Let us therefore come boldly to the throne of grace, that we may obtain mercy, and find grace to help in time of need.

HEBREWS 4:16

INSIGHTS ON FAITH FROM SMITH WIGGLESWORTH

I am moved only by what I believe. I know this: no man looks at the circumstances if he believes. No man relies on his feelings if he believes. The man who believes God has his request.

⌒

You will never find Jesus missing an opportunity to do good. You will find that He is always more willing to work than we are to give Him an opportunity to work. The trouble is that we do not come to Him; we do not ask Him for what He is more than willing to give.

⌒

The work is done if you only believe it. It is done. *"He Himself took our infirmities and bore our sicknesses"* (Matthew 8:17). If only you can see the Lamb of God going to Calvary! He took our flesh so that He could take upon Himself the full burden of all our sin and all the consequences of sin. There on the cross of Calvary, the results of sin were also dealt with.

GOD'S PRESENCE

And He said, My presence shall go with you, and I will give you rest.   EXODUS 33:14

Be strong and of a good courage, fear not, nor be afraid of them: for the LORD your God, He it is that does go with you; He will not fail you, nor forsake you.   DEUTERONOMY 31:6

For the LORD will not forsake His people for His great name's sake: because it has pleased the LORD to make you His people.
                                                    1 SAMUEL 12:22

The eyes of the LORD are upon the righteous, and His ears are open to their cry. …The righteous cry, and the LORD hears, and delivers them out of all their troubles.   PSALM 34:15, 17

Be still, and know that I am God: I will be exalted among the heathen, I will be exalted in the earth.   PSALM 46:10

He shall call upon Me, and I will answer him: I will be with him in trouble; I will deliver him, and honor him. With long life will I satisfy him, and show him My salvation.   PSALM 91:15–16

Fear you not; for I am with you: be not dismayed; for I am Your God: I will strengthen you; yea, I will help you; yea, I will uphold you with the right hand of My righteousness. ...I will open rivers in high places, and fountains in the midst of the valleys: I will make the wilderness a pool of water, and the dry land springs of water. ISAIAH 41:10, 18

Behold, I have graven you upon the palms of My hands; your walls are continually before Me. ISAIAH 49:16

And you shall seek Me, and find Me, when you shall search for Me with all your heart. JEREMIAH 29:13

For the mountains shall depart, and the hills be removed; but My kindness shall not depart from you, neither shall the covenant of My peace be removed, says the LORD that has mercy on you. ISAIAH 54:10

As the Father has loved Me, so have I loved you: continue you in My love. JOHN 15:9

These things I have spoken to you, that in Me you might have peace. In the world you shall have tribulation: but be of good cheer; I have overcome the world. JOHN 16:33

Who shall separate us from the love of Christ? shall tribulation, or distress, or persecution, or famine, or nakedness, or peril, or sword? …Nay, in all these things we are more than conquerors through Him that loved us. For I am persuaded, that neither death, nor life, nor angels, nor principalities, nor powers, nor things present, nor things to come, nor height, nor depth, nor any other creature, shall be able to separate us from the love of God, which is in Christ Jesus our Lord. ROMANS 8:35, 37–39

Draw near to God, and He will draw near to you. Cleanse your hands, you sinners; and purify your hearts, you double minded. JAMES 4:8

Behold, I stand at the door, and knock: if any man hear My voice, and open the door, I will come in to him, and will sup with him, and he with Me. REVELATION 3:20

INSIGHTS ON FAITH FROM SMITH WIGGLESWORTH

If the saints only knew how precious they are in the sight of God (see Isaiah 43:4), they would scarcely be able to sleep for thinking of His watchful, loving care. Oh, He is a precious Jesus! He is a lovely Savior! He is divine in all His attitudes toward us, and He makes our hearts burn. There is nothing like it.

⌒

He took our infirmities. He bore our sickness; He came to heal our brokenheartedness. Jesus wants us to come forth in divine likeness, in resurrection force, in the power of the Spirit, to walk in faith and understand His Word. That is what He meant when He said He would give us power over all the power of the Enemy. He will subdue all things until everything comes into perfect harmony with His will.

⌒

God does not want me to cry. God does not want me to labor. God does not want me to anguish and to be filled with anxiety and a sorrowful spirit. What does He want me to do? Only believe. After you have received, only believe. Come to the authority of it; dare to believe. Say, "I will do it!"

PROTECTION

And said, If you will diligently hearken to the voice of the LORD your God, and will do that which is right in His sight, and will give ear to His commandments, and keep all His statutes, I will put none of these diseases upon you, which I have brought upon the Egyptians: for I am the LORD that heals you.

EXODUS 15:26

And of Benjamin he said, The beloved of the LORD shall dwell in safety by him; and the LORD shall cover him all the day long, and he shall dwell between his shoulders.   DEUTERONOMY 33:12

I will both lay me down in peace, and sleep: for You, LORD, only make me dwell in safety.   PSALM 4:8

The angel of the LORD encamps round about them that fear Him, and delivers them.   PSALM 34:7

The LORD also will be a refuge for the oppressed, a refuge in times of trouble. And they that know Your name will put their trust in You: for You, LORD, have not forsaken them that seek You.

PSALM 9:9–10

Bless the LORD, O my soul: and all that is within me, bless His holy name. Bless the LORD, O my soul, and forget not all His benefits: who forgives all your iniquities; who heals all your diseases; who redeems your life from destruction; who crowns you with lovingkindness and tender mercies; who satisfies your mouth with good things; so that your youth is renewed like the eagle's.

PSALM 103:1–5

That it might be fulfilled which was spoken by Isaiah the prophet, saying, Himself took our infirmities, and bore our sicknesses.

MATTHEW 8:17

For verily I say to you, That whosoever shall say to this mountain, Be you removed, and be you cast into the sea; and shall not doubt in his heart, but shall believe that those things which he says shall come to pass; he shall have whatsoever he says. MARK 11:23

Therefore I say to you, What things soever you desire, when you pray, believe that you receive them, and you shall have them.

MARK 11:24

But when Jesus heard it, He answered him, saying, Fear not: believe only, and she shall be made whole. LUKE 8:50

How God anointed Jesus of Nazareth with the Holy Ghost and with power: who went about doing good, and healing all that were oppressed of the devil; for God was with Him. ACTS 10:38

Fight the good fight of faith, lay hold on eternal life, whereto you are also called, and have professed a good profession before many witnesses. 1 TIMOTHY 6:12

Wherefore take to you the whole armor of God, that you may be able to withstand in the evil day, and having done all, to stand. EPHESIANS 6:13

But let him ask in faith, nothing wavering. For he that wavers is like a wave of the sea driven with the wind and tossed. JAMES 1:6

And who is he that will harm you, if you be followers of that which is good? 1 PETER 3:13

INSIGHTS ON FAITH FROM SMITH WIGGLESWORTH

Why is Satan allowed to bring sickness? It is because we know better than we act. And if people would do as well as they know, they would have no sickness. If we would be true to our convictions and walk according to the light we have been given, God would verify His presence in the midst of us, and we would know that sickness cannot *"come near [our] dwelling; for He shall give His angels charge over you, to keep you in all your ways"* (Psalm 91:10–11).

⌇

If you ask God once for healing, you will get it. But if you ask a thousand times a day until you do not even know you are asking, you will get nothing. If you would ask God for your healing now and begin praising Him because He never breaks His word, you would go out of here perfect. *"Only believe"* (Mark 5:36).

⌇

The Word can drive every disease away from your body. Healing is your portion in Christ, who Himself is our bread, our life, our health, our All in All. Though you may be deep in sin, you can come to Him in repentance, and He will forgive and cleanse and heal you. His words are spirit and life to those who will receive them. (See John 6:63–64.)

"LEAVE DOUBTING STREET; LIVE ON FAITH-VICTORY STREET. JESUS SENT THE SEVENTY OUT, AND THEY CAME BACK IN VICTORY. IT TAKES GOD TO MAKE IT REAL. DARE TO BELIEVE UNTIL THERE IS NOT A SICK PERSON, UNTIL THERE IS NO SICKNESS, UNTIL EVERYTHING THAT IS NOT OF GOD IS WITHERED, AND THE LIFE OF JESUS IS IMPLANTED WITHIN."

—SMITH WIGGLESWORTH

5

JESUS' LIFE IN YOU

FINDING GOD DURING THE HARD TIMES

*For the L*ORD *your God brings you into a good land, a land of brooks of water, of fountains and depths that spring out of valleys and hills.*   D*EUTERONOMY* 8:7

Yea, though I walk through the valley of the shadow of death, I will fear no evil: for You are with me; Your rod and Your staff they comfort me.   P*SALM* 23:4

*Many are the afflictions of the righteous: but the L*ORD *delivers him out of them all.*   P*SALM* 34:19

*Behold, God is my salvation; I will trust, and not be afraid: for the L*ORD J*EHOVAH is my strength and my song; He also is become my salvation.*   I*SAIAH* 12:2

Say to them that are of a fearful heart, Be strong, fear not: behold, your God will come with vengeance, even God with a recompence; He will come and save you.   Isaiah 35:4

Who has measured the waters in the hollow of His hand, and meted out heaven with the span, and comprehended the dust of the earth in a measure, and weighed the mountains in scales, and the hills in a balance?   Isaiah 40:12

Fear you not; for I am with you: be not dismayed; for I am Your God: I will strengthen you; yea, I will help you; yea, I will uphold you with the right hand of My righteousness.   Isaiah 41:10

Every valley shall be filled, and every mountain and hill shall be brought low; and the crooked shall be made straight, and the rough ways shall be made smooth.   Luke 3:5

For the invisible things of Him from the creation of the world are clearly seen, being understood by the things that are made, even His eternal power and Godhead; so that they are without excuse.   Romans 1:20

And He said to me, My grace is sufficient for you: for My strength is made perfect in weakness. Most gladly therefore will I rather glory in my infirmities, that the power of Christ may rest upon me.   2 Corinthians 12:9

I know both how to be abased, and I know how to abound: every where and in all things I am instructed both to be full and to be hungry, both to abound and to suffer need. I can do all things through Christ which strengthens me.

PHILIPPIANS 4:12–13

If any of you lack wisdom, let him ask of God, that gives to all men liberally, and upbraids not; and it shall be given him.

JAMES 1:5

Beloved, think it not strange concerning the fiery trial which is to try you, as though some strange thing happened to you: but rejoice, inasmuch as you are partakers of Christ's sufferings; that, when His glory shall be revealed, you may be glad also with exceeding joy. 1 PETER 4:12–13

But the God of all grace, who has called us to His eternal glory by Christ Jesus, after that you have suffered a while, make you perfect, stablish, strengthen, settle you. 1 PETER 5:10

And God shall wipe away all tears from their eyes; and there shall be no more death, neither sorrow, nor crying, neither shall there be any more pain: for the former things are passed away.

REVELATION 21:4

INSIGHTS ON FAITH FROM SMITH WIGGLESWORTH

There is no dry place in God, but all good things come out of hard times. The harder the place you are in, the more blessing can come out of it as you yield to His plan. Oh, if only I had known God's plan in its fullness, I might never have had a tear in my life. God is so abundant, so full of love and mercy; there is no lack to those who trust in Him.

～

People come up to me all the time and say, "I have been prayed for, and I am just the same." It is enough to make you kick them. I don't mean that literally. I would be the last man to kick anybody in this place. God forbid. *"For the weapons of our warfare are not carnal but mighty in God for pulling down strongholds"* (2 Corinthians 10:4). But if I can get you enraged against the powers of darkness and the powers of disease, if I can wake you up, you won't go to bed unless you prove that there is a Master in you who is greater than the power that is hanging around you.

～

People miss the greatest plan of healing because of moving from one thing to another. Become stationary. God wants you to take the Word. Claim the Word. Believe it. That is the perfect way of healing: turn not to the right hand nor to the left, but believe God.

JESUS IS WITH US

Fear you not; for I am with you: be not dismayed; for I am Your God: I will strengthen you; yea, I will help you; yea, I will uphold you with the right hand of My righteousness.   Isaiah 41:10

All things were made by Him; and without Him was not any thing made that was made.   John 1:3

And the Word was made flesh, and dwelt among us, (and we beheld His glory, the glory as of the only begotten of the Father,) full of grace and truth.   John 1:14

I am the living bread which came down from heaven: if any man eat of this bread, he shall live for ever: and the bread that I will give is My flesh, which I will give for the life of the world.

John 6:51

Jesus said to them, Verily, verily, I say to you, Before Abraham was, I am.   John 8:58

I am the good shepherd: the good shepherd gives His life for the sheep.   John 10:11

No man takes it from Me, but I lay it down of Myself. I have power to lay it down, and I have power to take it again. This commandment have I received of My Father. JOHN 10:18

Jesus said to her, I am the resurrection, and the life: he that believes in Me, though he were dead, yet shall he live: and whosoever lives and believes in Me shall never die. Believe you this?
JOHN 11:25–26

Jesus says to him, I am the way, the truth, and the life: no man comes to the Father, but by Me. JOHN 14:6

I am the vine, you are the branches: He that abides in Me, and I in him, the same brings forth much fruit: for without Me you can do nothing. JOHN 15:5

You have not chosen Me, but I have chosen you, and ordained you, that you should go and bring forth fruit, and that your fruit should remain: that whatsoever you shall ask of the Father in My name, He may give it you. JOHN 15:16

For none of us lives to himself, and no man dies to himself. For whether we live, we live to the Lord; and whether we die, we die to the Lord: whether we live therefore, or die, we are the Lord's.
ROMANS 14:7–8

Wherefore God also has highly exalted Him, and given Him a name which is above every name: that at the name of Jesus every knee should bow, of things in heaven, and things in earth, and things under the earth; and that every tongue should confess that Jesus Christ is Lord, to the glory of God the Father.

PHILIPPIANS 2:9–11

For if we believe that Jesus died and rose again, even so them also which sleep in Jesus will God bring with Him.

1 THESSALONIANS 4:14

Who being the brightness of His glory, and the express image of His person, and upholding all things by the word of His power, when He had by Himself purged our sins, sat down on the right hand of the Majesty on high.　　　　HEBREWS 1:3

Who His own self bore our sins in His own body on the tree, that we, being dead to sins, should live to righteousness: by whose stripes you were healed.　　　　1 PETER 2:24

INSIGHTS ON FAITH FROM SMITH WIGGLESWORTH

"Keep on believing, Jesus is near,

Keep on believing, there's nothing to fear;

Keep on believing, this is the way,

Faith in the night, the same as the day."

⌇

Let's look at the following Scripture: *"Whatever you ask in My name, that I will do, that the Father may be glorified in the Son"* (John 14:13). If we ask anything in His name, He will do it! Who says this? Jesus—that blessed Jesus, that lovely Jesus, that Incarnation from heaven, that blessed Son of God. How He wants to bless!

⌇

See this helpless man at the pool. Jesus asked him, *"Do you want to be made well?"* (John 5:6). But there was a difficulty in the way. The man had one eye on the pool and one eye on Jesus. If you will look only to Christ and put both of your eyes on Him, you can be made every bit whole—spirit, soul, and body. It is the promise of the living God that those who believe are justified, made free, from all things. (See Acts 13:39.) And *"if the Son makes you free, you shall be free indeed"* (John 8:36).

JOY OF HEALING

But let all those that put their trust in You rejoice: let them ever shout for joy, because You defend them: let them also that love Your name be joyful in You. PSALM 5:11

For our heart shall rejoice in Him, because we have trusted in His holy name. PSALM 33:21

Make a joyful noise to the LORD, all you lands. Serve the LORD with gladness: come before His presence with singing.
PSALM 100:1–2

The LORD has done great things for us; whereof we are glad.
PSALM 126:3

They that sow in tears shall reap in joy. He that goes forth and weeps, bearing precious seed, shall doubtless come again with rejoicing, bringing his sheaves with him. PSALM 126:5–6

Therefore the redeemed of the LORD shall return, and come with singing to Zion; and everlasting joy shall be upon their head: they shall obtain gladness and joy; and sorrow and mourning shall flee away. ISAIAH 51:11

For you shall go out with joy, and be led forth with peace: the mountains and the hills shall break forth before you into singing, and all the trees of the field shall clap their hands.

ISAIAH 55:12

Until now have you asked nothing in My name: ask, and you shall receive, that your joy may be full. JOHN 16:24

These things I have spoken to you, that in Me you might have peace. In the world you shall have tribulation: but be of good cheer; I have overcome the world. JOHN 16:33

Rejoicing in hope; patient in tribulation; continuing instant in prayer. ROMANS 12:12

Rejoice in the Lord always: and again I say, Rejoice.

PHILIPPIANS 4:4

PROMISE OF LONG LIFE

And you shall serve the LORD *your God, and He shall bless your bread, and your water; and I will take sickness away from the midst of you. There shall nothing cast their young, nor be barren, in your land: the number of your days I will fulfill.*

EXODUS 23:25–26

You shall walk in all the ways which the LORD *your God has commanded you, that you may live, and that it may be well with you, and that you may prolong your days in the land which you shall possess.* DEUTERONOMY 5:33

And your age shall be clearer than the noonday: you shall shine forth, you shall be as the morning. JOB 11:17

LORD, make me to know my end, and the measure of my days, what it is: that I may know how frail I am. Behold, You have made my days as an handbreadth; and my age is as nothing before You: verily every man at his best state is altogether vanity.

PSALM 39:4–5

Cast me not off in the time of old age; forsake me not when my strength fails. PSALM 71:9

INSIGHTS ON FAITH FROM SMITH WIGGLESWORTH

You say, "Oh, if I could only believe!" Jesus understands. He knew that the helpless man had been in that condition for a long time. He is full of compassion. He knows about that kidney trouble; He knows about those corns; He knows about that neuralgia. There is nothing He does not know. He wants only a chance to show Himself merciful and gracious to you, but He wants to encourage you to believe Him. If you can only believe, you can be saved and healed.

Suppose you come for healing. You know as well as possible that, according to the natural life, there is no virtue in your body to give you that health. You also know that the ailment from which you suffer has so drained your life and energy that there is no help at all in you, but God says that you will be healed if you believe.

"Forever and ever, not for a day,
He keepeth His promise forever;
To all who believe,
To all who obey,
He keepeth His promise forever."

PROMISE OF LONG LIFE

O God, You have taught me from my youth: and presently have I declared Your wondrous works. Now also when I am old and grey-headed, O God, forsake me not; until I have showed Your strength to this generation, and Your power to every one that is to come. PSALM 71:17–18

With long life will I satisfy him, and show him My salvation. PSALM 91:16

I shall not die, but live, and declare the works of the LORD. PSALM 118:17

For by me your days shall be multiplied, and the years of your life shall be increased. PROVERBS 9:11

And even to your old age I am He; and even to hoar hairs will I carry you: I have made, and I will bear; even I will carry, and will deliver you. ISAIAH 46:4

Beloved, I wish above all things that you may prosper and be in health, even as your soul prospers. 3 JOHN 1:2

POWER OF PRAISE

Therefore I will give thanks to You, O Lord, among the heathen, and I will sing praises to Your name.   2 SAMUEL 22:50

The meek shall eat and be satisfied: they shall praise the Lord that seek Him: your heart shall live for ever.   PSALM 22:26

Bless the Lord, O my soul: and all that is within me, bless His holy name. Bless the Lord, O my soul, and forget not all His benefits.   PSALM 103:1–2

Praise you the Lord. O give thanks to the Lord; for He is good: for His mercy endures for ever. Who can utter the mighty acts of the Lord? who can show forth all His praise?   PSALM 106:1–2

Not to us, O Lord, not to us, but to Your name give glory, for Your mercy, and for Your truth's sake.   PSALM 115:1

Praise you the Lord. Praise God in His sanctuary: praise Him in the firmament of His power. Praise Him for His mighty acts: praise Him according to His excellent greatness. Praise Him with the sound of the trumpet: praise Him with the psaltery and harp. Praise Him with the timbrel and dance: praise Him with stringed instruments and organs. Praise Him upon the loud cymbals: praise Him upon the high sounding cymbals. Let every thing that has breath praise the Lord. Praise you the Lord.   PSALM 150:1–6

And Jesus looking upon them says, With men it is impossible, but not with God: for with God all things are possible.

MARK 10:27

And in that day you shall ask Me nothing. Verily, verily, I say to you, Whatsoever you shall ask the Father in My name, He will give it you.

JOHN 16:23

By Him therefore let us offer the sacrifice of praise to God continually, that is, the fruit of our lips giving thanks to His name.

HEBREWS 13:15

Is any among you afflicted? let him pray. Is any merry? let him sing psalms.

JAMES 5:13

You are a chosen generation, a royal priesthood, a holy nation, a peculiar people; that you should show forth the praises of Him who has called you out of darkness into His marvelous light.

1 PETER 2:9

INSIGHTS ON FAITH FROM SMITH WIGGLESWORTH

If you will allow Jesus to have charge of your bodies, you will find that this Spirit will quicken you and will free you. Talk about divine healing! You cannot remove it from the Scriptures. They are full of it. You will find, also, that all who are healed by the power of God, especially believers, will find their healing an incentive to make them purer and holier. If divine healing merely made the body whole, it would be worth very little. Divine healing is the marvelous act of the providence of God coming into your mortal bodies, and after being touched by the Almighty, can you ever remain the same? No. Like me, you will eagerly worship and serve God.

〜

When you begin to pour out your heart to God in love, your very being, your whole self, desires Him. Perfect love means that Jesus has taken hold of your intentions, desires, and thoughts and purified everything. Perfect love cannot fear. (See 1 John 4:18.)

POWER OF THE BLOOD

For the life of the flesh is in the blood: and I have given it to you upon the altar to make an atonement for your souls: for it is the blood that makes an atonement for the soul.   LEVITICUS 17:11

And, behold, there was a man which had his hand withered. And they asked Him, saying, Is it lawful to heal on the sabbath days? that they might accuse Him.   MATTHEW 12:10

In whom we have redemption through His blood, the forgiveness of sins, according to the riches of His grace.   EPHESIANS 1:77

Now the God of peace, that brought again from the dead our Lord Jesus, that great shepherd of the sheep, through the blood of the everlasting covenant, Make you perfect in every good work to do His will, working in you that which is wellpleasing in His sight, through Jesus Christ; to whom be glory for ever and ever. Amen.
HEBREWS 13:20–21

But if we walk in the light, as He is in the light, we have fellowship one with another, and the blood of Jesus Christ His Son cleanses us from all sin.   1 JOHN 1:7

POWER OF PRAYER

The eyes of the LORD *are upon the righteous, and His ears are open to their cry.* PSALM 34:15

The righteous cry, and the LORD *hears, and delivers them out of all their troubles.* PSALM 34:17

Evening, and morning, and at noon, will I pray, and cry aloud: and He shall hear my voice. PSALM 55:17

O You that hears prayer, to You shall all flesh come. PSALM 65:2

If I regard iniquity in my heart, the LORD *will not hear me.* PSALM 66:18

He shall call upon Me, and I will answer him: I will be with him in trouble; I will deliver him, and honor him. PSALM 91:15

I will offer to You the sacrifice of thanksgiving, and will call upon the name of the LORD. PSALM 116:17

Out of the depths have I cried to You, O LORD. *Lord, hear my voice: let Your ears be attentive to the voice of my supplications.* PSALM 130:1–2

The LORD is near to all them that call upon Him, to all that call upon Him in truth. He will fulfill the desire of them that fear Him: He also will hear their cry, and will save them.

PSALM 145:18–19

The LORD is far from the wicked: but He hears the prayer of the righteous.   PROVERBS 15:29

And it shall come to pass, that before they call, I will answer; and while they are yet speaking, I will hear.   ISAIAH 65:24

Then shall you call upon Me, and you shall go and pray to Me, and I will hearken to you.   JEREMIAH 29:12

If My people, which are called by My name, shall humble themselves and pray, and seek My face, and turn from their wicked ways; then I will hear from heaven, and will forgive their sin, and will heal their land.   2 CHRONICLES 7:14

INSIGHTS ON FAITH FROM SMITH WIGGLESWORTH

There is healing through the blood of Christ and deliverance for every captive. God never intended His children to live in misery because of some affliction that comes directly from the Devil. A perfect atonement was made at Calvary. I believe that Jesus bore my sins, and I am free from them all. I am justified from all things if I dare to believe. (See Acts 13:39.) *"He Himself took our infirmities and bore our sicknesses"* (Matthew 8:17), and if I dare to believe, I can be healed.

⌒

The precious blood of the Lord Jesus Christ is effective; right now it will cleanse your heart and put this life, this wonderful life of God, within you. The blood will make you every bit whole if you dare to believe.

POWER OF PRAYER

Call to Me, and I will answer you, and show you great and mighty things, which you know not.   Jeremiah 33:3

Be not you therefore like to them: for your Father knows what things you have need of, before you ask Him.   Matthew 6:8

After this manner therefore pray you: Our Father which is in heaven, hallowed be Your name. Your kingdom come, Your will be done in earth, as it is in heaven. Give us this day our daily bread. And forgive us our debts, as we forgive our debtors. And lead us not into temptation, but deliver us from evil: for Yours is the kingdom, and the power, and the glory, for ever. Amen.
Matthew 6:9–13

Again I say to you, That if two of you shall agree on earth as touching any thing that they shall ask, it shall be done for them of My Father which is in heaven. For where two or three are gathered together in My name, there am I in the midst of them.
Matthew 18:19–20

Therefore I say to you, What things soever you desire, when you pray, believe that you receive them, and you shall have them.
Mark 11:24

And whatsoever you shall ask in My name, that will I do, that the Father may be glorified in the Son. If you shall ask any thing in My name, I will do it. JOHN 14:13–14

If you abide in Me, and My words abide in you, you shall ask what you will, and it shall be done to you. JOHN 15:7

And in that day you shall ask Me nothing. Verily, verily, I say to you, Whatsoever you shall ask the Father in My name, He will give it you. Until now have you asked nothing in My name: ask, and you shall receive, that your joy may be full.

JOHN 16:23–24

Is any among you afflicted? let him pray. Is any merry? let him sing psalms. JAMES 5:13

Confess your faults one to another, and pray one for another, that ye may be healed. The effectual fervent prayer of a righteous man avails much. JAMES 5:16

SICKNESS AND DISEASE

And you shall serve the LORD your God, and He shall bless your bread, and your water; and I will take sickness away from the midst of you.   EXODUS 23:25

His flesh shall be fresher than a child's: he shall return to the days of his youth.   JOB 33:25

The LORD is my light and my salvation; whom shall I fear? the LORD is the strength of my life; of whom shall I be afraid? When the wicked, even my enemies and my foes, came upon me to eat up my flesh, they stumbled and fell. Though a host should encamp against me, my heart shall not fear: though war should rise against me, in this will I be confident.   PSALM 27:1–3

There shall no evil befall you, neither shall any plague come near your dwelling.   PSALM 91:10

Who forgives all your iniquities; who heals all your diseases.
                                                        PSALM 103:3

He sent His word, and healed them, and delivered them from their destructions.   PSALM 107:20

INSIGHTS ON FAITH FROM SMITH WIGGLESWORTH

If you can only believe, you can be saved and healed right now. Dare to believe that Jesus was wounded for your transgressions, was bruised for your iniquities, was chastised that you might have peace, and that by His stripes there is healing for you here and now. (See Isaiah 53:5.) You have suffered and failed because you have not believed Him. Cry out to Him even now, *"Lord, I believe; help my unbelief!"* (Mark 9:24).

⌒

We have in this precious Word a real basis for the truth of healing. In these verses God gives very definite instructions to the sick. If you are sick, your part is to call for the elders of the church; it is their part to anoint and pray for you in faith. Then the whole situation rests with the Lord. When you have been anointed and prayed for, you can rest assured that the Lord will raise you up. It is the Word of God.

SICKNESS AND DISEASE

I shall not die, but live, and declare the works of the LORD.

PSALM 118:17

I will praise You; for I am fearfully and wonderfully made: marvellous are Your works; and that my soul knows right well.

PSALM 139:14

My son, attend to my words; incline your ear to my sayings. Let them not depart from your eyes; keep them in the midst of your heart. For they are life to those that find them, and health to all their flesh. Proverbs 4:20–22

The light of the eyes rejoices the heart: and a good report makes the bones fat. PROVERBS 15:30

But He was wounded for our transgressions, He was bruised for our iniquities: the chastisement of our peace was upon Him; and with His stripes we are healed. ISAIAH 53:5

Heal me, O LORD, *and I shall be healed; save me, and I shall be saved: for You art my praise.* JEREMIAH 17:14

For I will restore health to You, and I will heal you of your wounds, says the LORD; *because they called you an outcast, saying, This is Zion, whom no man seeks after.* JEREMIAH 30:17

Behold, I will bring it health and cure, and I will cure them, and will reveal to them the abundance of peace and truth.

JEREMIAH 33:6

The hand of the LORD was upon me, and carried me out in the Spirit of the LORD, and set me down in the midst of the valley which was full of bones, and caused me to pass by them round about: and, behold, there were very many in the open valley; and, lo, they were very dry. And He said to me, Son of man, can these bones live? And I answered, O Lord GOD, You know. Again He said to me, Prophesy upon these bones, and say to them, O you dry bones, hear the word of the LORD!   EZEKIEL 37:1–4

And when He was come into the house, the blind men came to Him: and Jesus says to them, Believe you that I am able to do this? They said to Him, Yea, Lord. Then touched He their eyes, saying, According to your faith be it to you. And their eyes were opened; and Jesus strictly charged them, saying, See that no man know it.

MATTHEW 9:28–30

And when Jesus saw her, He called her to Him, and said to her, Woman, you are loosed from your infirmity.   LUKE 13:12

Is any sick among you? let him call for the elders of the church; and let them pray over him, anointing him with oil in the name of the Lord: And the prayer of faith shall save the sick, and the Lord shall raise him up; and if he have committed sins, they shall be forgiven him. Confess your faults one to another, and pray one for another, that you may be healed. The effectual fervent prayer of a righteous man avails much.　　　JAMES 5:14–16

Who His own self bore our sins in His own body on the tree, that we, being dead to sins, should live to righteousness: by whose stripes you were healed.　　　1 PETER 2:24

INSIGHTS ON FAITH FROM SMITH WIGGLESWORTH

So many are trying drugs, quacks, pills, and plasters. You will find that if you dare trust God, He will never fail. *"The prayer of faith will save the sick, and the Lord will raise him up"* (James 5:15). Do you trust Him? He is worthy to be trusted.

⌣

Today there is bread—there is life and health—for every child of God through His powerful Word. The Word can drive every disease away from your body. Healing is your portion in Christ, who Himself is our bread, our life, our health, our All in All. Though you may be deep in sin, you can come to Him in repentance, and He will forgive and cleanse and heal you.

⌣

The power of God is just the same today as it was in the past. Men need to be taken back to the old paths, to the old-time faith, to believing God's Word and every *"Thus says the Lord"* in it. The Spirit of the Lord is moving in these days. God is coming forth. If you want to be in the rising tide, "you must accept all God has said."

"GOD IS A REALITY, AND HIS POWER CAN NEVER FAIL. AS OUR FAITH REACHES OUT, GOD WILL MEET US, AND THE SAME RAIN WILL FALL. IT IS THE SAME BLOOD THAT CLEANSES, THE SAME POWER, THE SAME HOLY SPIRIT, AND THE SAME JESUS MADE REAL THROUGH THE POWER OF THE HOLY SPIRIT! WHAT WOULD HAPPEN IF WE WOULD BELIEVE GOD?"

—SMITH WIGGLESWORTH

6

THE LORD HEALS

PROMISE OF HEALING

And said, If you will diligently hearken to the voice of the LORD your God, and will do that which is right in His sight, and will give ear to His commandments, and keep all His statutes, I will put none of these diseases upon you, which I have brought upon the Egyptians: for I am the LORD that heals you .

EXODUS 15:26

And the LORD will take away from you all sickness, and will put none of the evil diseases of Egypt, which you know, upon you; but will lay them upon all them that hate you. DEUTERONOMY 7:15

The LORD make His face shine upon you, and be gracious to you: The LORD lift up His countenance upon you, and give you peace. And they shall put My name upon the children of Israel, and I will bless them. NUMBERS 6:25–27

And Moses cried to the LORD, saying, Heal her now, O God, I beseech you. NUMBERS 12:13

HEALING PSALMS

Have mercy on me, O Lord; for I am weak: O Lord, heal me; for my bones are vexed. PSALM 6:2

My soul is also sore vexed: but You, O Lord, how long? Return, O Lord, deliver my soul: oh save me for Your mercies' sake.
PSALM 6:3–4

O Lord my God, I cried to You, and You have healed me. O Lord, You have brought up my soul from the grave: You have kept me alive, that I should not go down to the pit.
PSALM 30:2–3

Have mercy upon me, O Lord, for I am in trouble: my eye is consumed with grief, yea, my soul and my belly. PSALM 31:9

He keeps all his bones: not one of them is broken. PSALM 34:20

This poor man cried, and the Lord heard him, and saved him out of all his troubles. PSALM 34:6

Let them shout for joy, and be glad, that favor my righteous cause: yea, let them say continually, Let the Lord be magnified, which has pleasure in the prosperity of His servant. PSALM 35:27

Blessed is he that considers the poor: the LORD will deliver him in time of trouble. The LORD will preserve him, and keep him alive; and he shall be blessed upon the earth: and You will not deliver him to the will of his enemies. The LORD will strengthen him upon the bed of languishing: You will make all his bed in his sickness.   PSALM 41:1–2

The LORD will strengthen him upon the bed of languishing: You will make all his bed in his sickness. I said, LORD, be merciful to me: heal my soul; for I have sinned against You.

PSALM 41:3–4

Why are you cast down, O my soul? and why are you disquieted in me? hope you in God: for I shall yet praise Him for the help of his countenance.   PSALM 42:5

Bless the LORD, O my soul, and forget not all His benefits: who forgives all your iniquities; who heals all your diseases; who redeems your life from destruction; who crowns you with lovingkindness and tender mercies.   PSALM 103:2–4

INSIGHTS ON FAITH FROM SMITH WIGGLESWORTH

God has you on this earth for the purpose of bringing out His character in you. He wants to destroy the power of the Devil. He wants to move you so that in the face of difficulties and hardships, you will praise the Lord. *"Count it all joy"* (James 1:2). You have to take a leap today; you have to leap into the promises. You have to believe that God never fails you; you have to believe it is impossible for God to break His word. He is *"from everlasting to everlasting"* (Psalm 90:2).

～

For if you really believe, you will ask God only once, and that is all you need, because He has abundance for your every need. But if you go right in the face of asking once and ask six times, He knows very well you do not mean what you ask, so you do not get it. God does not honor unbelief; He honors faith.

HEALING PSALMS

Yet sets He the poor on high from affliction, and makes him families like a flock.   PSALM 107:41

It is good for me that I have been afflicted; that I might learn Your statutes.   PSALM 119:71

I am afflicted very much: quicken me, O LORD, according to Your word.   PSALM 119:107

Unless Your law had been my delights, I should then have perished in my affliction. I will never forget Your precepts: for with them You have quickened me. I am Yours, save me: for I have sought Your precepts. The wicked have waited for me to destroy me: but I will consider Your testimonies.   PSALM 119:92–95

Trouble and anguish have taken hold on me: yet Your commandments are my delights. The righteousness of Your testimonies is everlasting: give me understanding, and I shall live.

PSALM 119:143–144

He heals the broken in heart, and binds up their wounds.

PSALM 147:3

HEALING WISDOM

Trust in the LORD with all your heart; and lean not to your own understanding. In all your ways acknowledge Him, and He shall direct your paths. Be not wise in your own eyes: fear the LORD, and depart from evil. It shall be health to your navel, and marrow to your bones.   PROVERBS 3:5–8

Pleasant words are as a honeycomb, sweet to the soul, and health to the bones.   PROVERBS 16:24

A merry heart does good like a medicine: but a broken spirit dries the bones.   PROVERBS 17:22

The spirit of a man will sustain his infirmity; but a wounded spirit who can bear?   PROVERBS 18:14

To every thing there is a season, and a time to every purpose under the heaven: a time to be born, and a time to die; a time to plant, and a time to pluck up that which is planted; a time to kill, and a time to heal; a time to break down, and a time to build up.

ECCLESIASTES 3:1–3

And he said, Go, and tell this people, Hear you indeed, but under-stand not; and see you indeed, but perceive not. Make the heart of this people fat, and make their ears heavy, and shut their eyes; lest they see with their eyes, and hear with their ears, and understand with their heart, and convert, and be healed. ISAIAH 6:9–10

And it shall come to pass in that day, that his burden shall be taken away from off your shoulder, and his yoke from off your neck, and the yoke shall be destroyed because of the anointing. ISAIAH 10:27

And the LORD *shall smite Egypt: He shall smite and heal it: and they shall return even to the* LORD, *and He shall be entreated of them, and shall heal them.* ISAIAH 19:22

Surely He has borne our griefs, and carried our sorrows: yet we did esteem Him stricken, smitten of God, and afflicted. But He was wounded for our transgressions, He was bruised for our iniq-uities: the chastisement of our peace was upon Him; and with His stripes we are healed. ISAIAH 53:4–5

All we like sheep have gone astray; we have turned every one to his own way; and the LORD *has laid on Him the iniquity of us all.* ISAIAH 53:6

INSIGHTS ON FAITH FROM SMITH WIGGLESWORTH

Every trial is to bring you to a greater position in God. The trial that tries your faith will take you on to the place where you will know that the faith of God will be forthcoming in the next test. No man is able to win any victory except through the power of the risen Christ within him.

⌇

Jesus is always willing to come and heal. He longs to help the sick ones. He loves to heal them of their afflictions. The Lord is healing many people today by means of handkerchiefs, even as He did in the days of Paul.

HEALING WISDOM

No weapon that is formed against you shall prosper; and every tongue that shall rise against you in judgment you shall condemn. This is the heritage of the servants of the LORD, and their righteousness is of Me, says the LORD.   ISAIAH 54:17

For as the rain comes down, and the snow from heaven, and returns not there, but waters the earth, and makes it bring forth and bud, that it may give seed to the sower, and bread to the eater: So shall My word be that goes forth out of My mouth: it shall not return to Me void, but it shall accomplish that which I please, and it shall prosper in the thing whereto I sent it.   ISAIAH 55:10–11

I have seen his ways, and will heal him: I will lead him also, and restore comforts to him and to his mourners. I create the fruit of the lips; Peace, peace to him that is far off, and to him that is near, says the LORD; and I will heal him.   ISAIAH 57:18–19

And when He had called to Him His twelve disciples, He gave them power against unclean spirits, to cast them out, and to heal all manner of sickness and all manner of disease.
                                           MATTHEW 10:1

Heal the sick, cleanse the lepers, raise the dead, cast out devils: freely you have received, freely give.   MATTHEW 10:8

Come to Me, all you that labor and are heavy laden, and I will give you rest. MATTHEW 11:28

Then says He to the man, Stretch forth your hand. And he stretched it forth; and it was restored whole, like as the other. MATTHEW 12:13

For this people's heart is waxed gross, and their ears are dull of hearing, and their eyes they have closed; lest at any time they should see with their eyes and hear with their ears, and should understand with their heart, and should be converted, and I should heal them. MATTHEW 13:15

And He did not many mighty works there because of their unbelief. MATTHEW 13:58

And Jesus went forth, and saw a great multitude, and was moved with compassion toward them, and He healed their sick. MATTHEW 14:14

And all things, whatsoever you shall ask in prayer, believing, you shall receive. MATTHEW 21:22

*And Jesus went about all Galilee, teaching in their synagogues,
and preaching the gospel of the kingdom, and healing all manner
of sickness and all manner of disease among the people. And His
fame went throughout all Syria: and they brought to Him all sick
people that were taken with divers diseases and torments, and
those which were possessed with devils, and those which were
lunatic, and those that had the palsy; and He healed them.*

MATTHEW 4:23–24

*When the evening was come, they brought to Him many that
were possessed with devils: and He cast out the spirits with His
word, and healed all that were sick: that it might be fulfilled which
was spoken by Isaiah the prophet, saying, Himself took our infirmities, and bore our sicknesses.*   MATTHEW 8:16–17

*And, behold, a woman, which was diseased with an issue of blood
twelve years, came behind Him, and touched the hem of His garment.*   MATTHEW 9:20

INSIGHTS ON FAITH FROM SMITH WIGGLESWORTH

All disease and weakness must go at the rebuke of the Master. God enables us to bind the Enemy and set the captive free.

❦

I say, brother and sister, unless God brings us into a place of brokenness of spirit, unless God remolds us in the great plan of His will for us, the best of us will utterly fail. But when we are absolutely taken in hand by the almighty God, God turns even our weakness into strength. He makes even that barren, helpless, groaning cry come forth, so that men and women are reborn in the travail. There is a place where our helplessness is touched by the power of God and where we come out shining as *"gold refined in the fire"* (Revelation 3:18).

❦

The Word gives life, and God wants there to be such life in you that you will be moved as it is preached. Oh, it is lovely to think that God can change things in a moment, and can heal in a moment. When God begins, who can hinder Him?

HEALING WISDOM

And when Jesus departed from there, two blind men followed Him, crying, and saying, You son of David, have mercy on us.

MATTHEW 9:27

And Jesus went about all the cities and villages, teaching in their synagogues, and preaching the gospel of the kingdom, and healing every sickness and every disease among the people.

MATTHEW 9:35

But Simon's wife's mother lay sick of a fever, and anon they tell Him of her. And He came and took her by the hand, and lifted her up; and immediately the fever left her, and she ministered to them.

MARK 1:30–31

And He said to her, Daughter, your faith has made you whole; go in peace, and be whole of your plague.

MARK 5:34

The Spirit of the Lord is upon Me, because He has anointed Me to preach the gospel to the poor; He has sent me to heal the bro-kenhearted, to preach deliverance to the captives, and recovering of sight to the blind, to set at liberty them that are bruised.

LUKE 4:18

Now when the sun was setting, all they that had any sick with divers diseases brought them to Him; and He laid His hands on every one of them, and healed them.   LUKE 4:40

But so much the more went there a fame abroad of Him: and great multitudes came together to hear, and to be healed by Him of their infirmities.   LUKE 5:15

And it came to pass on a certain day, as He was teaching, that there were Pharisees and doctors of the law sitting by, which were come out of every town of Galilee, and Judaea, and Jerusalem: and the power of the Lord was present to heal them.   LUKE 5:17

And when the Lord saw her, He had compassion on her, and said to her, Weep not.   LUKE 7:13

And in that same hour He cured many of their infirmities and plagues, and of evil spirits; and to many that were blind He gave sight.   LUKE 7:21

Wherefore neither thought I myself worthy to come to You: but say in a word, and my servant shall be healed.   LUKE 7:7

And certain women, which had been healed of evil spirits and infirmities, Mary called Magdalene, out of whom went seven devils.　　　　　　　　　　　　　　　　　LUKE 8:2

And He said to her, Daughter, be of good comfort: your faith has made you whole; go in peace.　　　　　　　　　LUKE 8:48

And heal the sick that are therein, and say to them, The kingdom of God is come near to you.　　　　　　　　　　LUKE 10:9

And the seventy returned again with joy, saying, Lord, even the devils are subject to us through Your name.　　　LUKE 10:17

Confess your faults to one another, and pray one for another, that you may be healed. The effectual fervent prayer of a righteous man avails much.　　　　　　　　　　　　　JAMES 5:16

INSIGHTS ON FAITH FROM SMITH WIGGLESWORTH

When faith lays hold, impossibilities must yield. When we touch the Divine and believe God, sin will drop off; disease will go; circumstances will change.

~

The divine gifts of healing are so profound in the person who has them that there is no such thing as doubt, and there could not be; whatever happens could not change the person's opinion or thought or act. He expects the very thing that God intends him to have as he lays hands upon the seeker.

~

When the woman who had suffered for twelve years from a flow of blood was healed, Jesus perceived that power had gone out of Him. (See Mark 5:25–34.) The woman's faith reached out, and His power was imparted. Immediately, the woman's being was charged with life, and her weakness departed. The conveying of this power produces everything you need, but it comes only as your faith reaches out to accept it. Faith is the victory. If you can believe, the healing power is yours.

HEALING WISDOM

Behold, I give to you power to tread on serpents and scorpions, and over all the power of the enemy: and nothing shall by any means hurt you. Notwithstanding in this rejoice not, that the spirits are subject to you; but rather rejoice, because your names are written in heaven. LUKE 10:19–20

And, behold, there was a woman which had a spirit of infirmity eighteen years, and was bowed together, and could in no wise lift up herself. And when Jesus saw her, He called her to Him, and said to her, Woman, you are loosed from your infirmity. And He laid His hands on her: and immediately she was made straight, and glorified God. LUKE 13:11–13

And they held their peace. And He took him, and healed him, and let him go. LUKE 14:4

Then said Jesus, Father, forgive them; for they know not what they do. And they parted His raiment, and cast lots. LUKE 23:34

And the Word was made flesh, and dwelt among us, (and we beheld His glory, the glory as of the only begotten of the Father,) full of grace and truth. JOHN 1:14

The next day John sees Jesus coming to him, and says, Behold the Lamb of God, which takes away the sin of the world.

JOHN 1:29

When he heard that Jesus was come out of Judaea into Galilee, he went to Him, and besought Him that He would come down, and heal his son: for he was at the point of death.   JOHN 4:47

And a certain man was there, which had an infirmity thirty and eight years. When Jesus saw him lie, and knew that he had been now a long time in that case, He says to him, Will you be made whole?   JOHN 5:5–6

Afterward Jesus finds him in the temple, and said to him, Behold, you are made whole: sin no more, lest a worse thing come to you.

JOHN 5:14

And you shall know the truth, and the truth shall make you free.

JOHN 8:32

Jesus answered, Neither has this man sinned, nor his parents: but that the works of God should be made manifest in him.

JOHN 9:3

The thief comes not, but for to steal, and to kill, and to destroy: I am come that they might have life, and that they might have it more abundantly. JOHN 10:10

Jesus said to her, I am the resurrection, and the life: he that believes in Me, though he were dead, yet shall he live: and whosoever lives and believes in Me shall never die. Believe you this?

JOHN 11:25–26

He has blinded their eyes, and hardened their heart; that they should not see with their eyes, nor understand with their heart, and be converted, and I should heal them. JOHN 12:40

Peace I leave with you, My peace I give to you: not as the world gives, give I to you. Let not your heart be troubled, neither let it be afraid. JOHN 14:27

INSIGHTS ON FAITH FROM SMITH WIGGLESWORTH

The Holy Spirit then makes Jesus King in your life; you regard Him as Lord and Master over all things, and you become submissive to Him in all things. You are not afraid to say, "You are mine! I love You!"

〜

I love Him. He is so beautiful; He is so sweet; He is so loving; He is so kind! He never turns a deaf ear; He never leaves you in distress. He heals brokenheartedness; He liberates the captive; and for those who are down and out, He comes right into that place and lifts the burden.

〜

"Faith is the substance of things hoped for" (Hebrews 11:1) right here in this life. It is here that God wants us to share in His divine nature. It is nothing less than the life of the Lord Himself imparted and flowing into our whole beings, so that our very bodies are quickened, so that every tissue, every drop of blood, and our bones, joints, and marrow receive this divine life.

〜

If God is with you and you know it, be in earnest. Pray and believe: *"Hold fast the confidence and the rejoicing of the hope firm to the end"* (Hebrews 3:6).

HEALING ENCOURAGEMENT

By stretching forth Your hand to heal; and that signs and wonders may be done by the name of Your holy child Jesus.   Acts 4:30

And Peter said to him, Aeneas, Jesus Christ makes you whole: arise, and make your bed. And he arose immediately.
Acts 9:34

How God anointed Jesus of Nazareth with the Holy Ghost and with power: who went about doing good, and healing all that were oppressed of the devil; for God was with Him.   Acts 10:38

And God wrought special miracles by the hands of Paul: so that from his body were brought to the sick handkerchiefs or aprons, and the diseases departed from them, and the evil spirits went out of them.   Acts 19:11–12

For the heart of this people is waxed gross, and their ears are dull of hearing, and their eyes have they closed; lest they should see with their eyes, and hear with their ears, and understand with their heart, and should be converted, and I should heal them.
Acts 28:27

Whom God has set forth to be a propitiation through faith in His blood, to declare His righteousness for the remission of sins that are past, through the forbearance of God.   Romans 3:25

Who was delivered for our offences, and was raised again for our justification. ROMANS 4:25

And not only so, but we glory in tribulations also: knowing that tribulation works patience; and patience, experience; and experience, hope: and hope makes not ashamed; because the love of God is shed abroad in our hearts by the Holy Ghost which is given to us. ROMANS 5:3–5

For when we were yet without strength, in due time Christ died for the ungodly. For scarcely for a righteous man will one die: yet perhaps for a good man some would even dare to die. But God commends His love toward us, in that, while we were yet sinners, Christ died for us. Much more then, being now justified by His blood, we shall be saved from wrath through Him. For if, when we were enemies, we were reconciled to God by the death of His Son, much more, being reconciled, we shall be saved by His life. ROMANS 5:6–10

I speak after the manner of men because of the infirmity of your flesh: for as you have yielded your members servants to uncleanness and to iniquity to iniquity; even so now yield your members servants to righteousness to holiness. ROMANS 6:19

For what the law could not do, in that it was weak through the flesh, God sending His own Son in the likeness of sinful flesh, and for sin, condemned sin in the flesh.　　　　　ROMANS 8:3

Likewise the Spirit also helps our infirmities: for we know not what we should pray for as we ought: but the Spirit itself makes intercession for us with groanings which cannot be uttered.
ROMANS 8:26

I beseech you therefore, brethren, by the mercies of God, that you present your bodies a living sacrifice, holy, acceptable to God, which is your reasonable service. And be not conformed to this world: but be you transformed by the renewing of your mind, that you may prove what is that good, and acceptable, and perfect, will of God.　　　　　ROMANS 12:1–2

We then that are strong ought to bear the infirmities of the weak, and not to please ourselves.　　　　　ROMANS 15:1

INSIGHTS ON FAITH FROM SMITH WIGGLESWORTH

I have seen some who had been suffering for years, but when they have been filled with the Holy Spirit, every bit of their sickness has passed away. The Spirit of God has made real to them the life of Jesus, and they have been completely liberated from every sickness and infirmity.

∽

Oh, if we only knew Jesus! One touch of His might meets the need of every crooked thing. The trouble is getting people to believe Him. The simplicity of this salvation is so wonderful. One touch of living faith in Him is all that is required for wholeness to be your portion.

HEALING ENCOURAGEMENT

To another faith by the same Spirit; to another the gifts of healing by the same Spirit.   1 CORINTHIANS 12:9

For I delivered to you first of all that which I also received, how that Christ died for our sins according to the scriptures.
                    1 CORINTHIANS 15:3

For which cause we faint not; but though our outward man perish, yet the inward man is renewed day by day. For our light affliction, which is but for a moment, works for us a far more exceeding and eternal weight of glory; while we look not at the things which are seen, but at the things which are not seen: for the things which are seen are temporal; but the things which are not seen are eternal.
                    2 CORINTHIANS 4:16–18

If I must needs glory, I will glory of the things which concern my infirmities.   2 CORINTHIANS 11:30

Of such an one will I glory: yet of myself I will not glory, but in my infirmities.   2 CORINTHIANS 12:5

Therefore I take pleasure in infirmities, in reproaches, in necessities, in persecutions, in distresses for Christ's sake: for when I am weak, then am I strong.   2 CORINTHIANS 12:10

And He said to me, My grace is sufficient for you: for My strength is made perfect in weakness. Most gladly therefore will I rather glory in my infirmities, that the power of Christ may rest upon me. 2 CORINTHIANS 12:9

For indeed he was sick near to death: but God had mercy on him; and not on him only, but on me also, lest I should have sorrow upon sorrow. PHILIPPIANS 2:27

For we have not an high priest which cannot be touched with the feeling of our infirmities; but was in all points tempted like as we are, yet without sin. HEBREWS 4:15

Who can have compassion on the ignorant, and on them that are out of the way; for that he himself also is compassed with infirmity. HEBREWS 5:2

Is any sick among you? let him call for the elders of the church; and let them pray over him, anointing him with oil in the name of the Lord: and the prayer of faith shall save the sick, and the Lord shall raise him up; and if he have committed sins, they shall be forgiven him. JAMES 5:14–15

Forasmuch as you know that you were not redeemed with corruptible things, as silver and gold, from your vain conversation received by tradition from your fathers; but with the precious blood of Christ, as of a lamb without blemish and without spot: who verily was foreordained before the foundation of the world, but was manifest in these last times for you, who by Him do believe in God, that raised Him up from the dead, and gave Him glory; that your faith and hope might be in God.

1 P<small>ETER</small> 1:18–21

But if we walk in the light, as He is in the light, we have fellowship one with another, and the blood of Jesus Christ His Son cleanses us from all sin. 1 J<small>OHN</small> 1:7

And whatsoever we ask, we receive of Him, because we keep His commandments, and do those things that are pleasing in His sight. And this is His commandment, That we should believe on the name of His Son Jesus Christ, and love one another, as He gave us commandment. 1 J<small>OHN</small> 3:22–23

INSIGHTS ON FAITH FROM SMITH WIGGLESWORTH

The Lord does not heal you to go to a baseball game or to a racetrack. He heals you for His glory so that from that moment your life will glorify Him.

Many people make vows to God in times of great crisis in their lives but fail to keep their vows, and in the end they become spiritually bankrupt. Blessed is the man *"who swears to his own hurt and does not change"* (Psalm 15:4), who keeps the vow he has made to God, who is willing to lay his all at God's feet. The man who does this never becomes a lean soul. God has promised to *"strengthen* [his] *bones"* (Isaiah 58:11). There is no dry place for such a man. He is always *"fresh and flourishing"* (Psalm 92:14), and he becomes stronger and stronger. It pays to trust God with all and to hold back nothing.

All things are naked and open to the eyes of Him with whom we are connected. (See Hebrews 4:13.) He knows about that asthma. He knows about that rheumatism. He knows about that pain in the back, head, or feet. He wants to loose every captive and to set you free just as He has set me free.

"MANY PEOPLE RECEIVE NO BLESSING BECAUSE THEY DID NOT THANK GOD FOR THE LAST BLESSING. A THANKFUL HEART IS A RECEIVING HEART. GOD WANTS TO KEEP YOU IN THE PLACE OF CONSTANT BELIEVING. KEEP ON BELIEVING, JESUS IS NEAR, KEEP ON BELIEVING, THERE'S NOTHING TO FEAR; KEEP ON BELIEVING, THIS IS THE WAY, FAITH IN THE NIGHT, THE SAME AS THE DAY."

—SMITH WIGGLESWORTH

7

COMFORT FOR EVERY NEED

PROMISE OF COMFORT

And he believed in the LORD; and He counted it to him for right-eousness. GENESIS 15:6

But the LORD said to Samuel, Look not on his countenance, or on the height of his stature; because I have refused him: for the LORD sees not as man sees; for man looks on the outward appearance, but the Lord looks on the heart. 1 SAMUEL 16:7

The God of my rock; in Him will I trust: He is my shield, and the horn of my salvation, my high tower, and my refuge, my savior; You save me from violence. 2 SAMUEL 22:3

To set up on high those that be low; that those which mourn may be exalted to safety. JOB 5:11

But I would strengthen you with my mouth, and the moving of my lips should assuage your grief. JOB 16:5

Blessed is the man that walks not in the counsel of the ungodly, nor stands in the way of sinners, nor sits in the seat of the scornful. But his delight is in the law of the Lord; *and in His law does he meditate day and night. And he shall be like a tree planted by the rivers of water, that brings forth his fruit in his season; his leaf also shall not wither; and whatsoever he does shall prosper. The ungodly are not so: but are like the chaff which the wind drives away. Therefore the ungodly shall not stand in the judgment, nor sinners in the congregation of the righteous. For the* Lord *knows the way of the righteous: but the way of the ungodly shall perish.*

Psalm 1:1–6

The Lord *also will be a refuge for the oppressed, a refuge in times of trouble. And they that know Your name will put their trust in You: for You,* Lord, *have not forsaken them that seek you.*

Psalm 9:9–10

Our fathers trusted in You: they trusted, and You did deliver them. They cried to You, and were delivered: they trusted in You, and were not confounded.

Psalm 22:4–5

*The L*ORD *is my shepherd; I shall not want. He makes me to lie down in green pastures: He leads me beside the still waters. He restores my soul: He leads me in the paths of righteousness for His name's sake. Yea, though I walk through the valley of the shadow of death, I will fear no evil: for You are with me; Your rod and Your staff they comfort me. You prepare a table before me in the presence of my enemies: You anoint my head with oil; my cup runs over. Surely goodness and mercy shall follow me all the days of my life: and I will dwell in the house of the L*ORD *for ever.*

PSALM 23:1–6

You are my hiding place; You shall preserve me from trouble; You shall compass me about with songs of deliverance.   PSALM 32:7

*The counsel of the L*ORD *stands for ever, the thoughts of His heart to all generations.*   PSALM 33:11

*Your mercy, O L*ORD*, is in the heavens; and Your faithfulness reaches to the clouds.*   PSALM 36:5

INSIGHTS ON FAITH FROM SMITH WIGGLESWORTH

The psalmist said, *"Before I was afflicted I went astray, but now I keep Your word"* (Psalm 119:67). And again, *"It is good for me that I have been afflicted, that I may learn Your statutes."* If our afflictions will bring us to the place where we see that we cannot *"live by bread alone, but by every word that proceeds from the mouth of God"* (Matthew 4:4), they will have served a blessed purpose. I want you to realize that there is a life of purity, a life made clean through the Word He has spoken, in which, through faith, you can glorify God with a body that is free from sickness, as well as with a spirit set free from satanic bondage.

Faith is just the open door through which the Lord comes. Do not say, "I was saved by faith" or "I was healed by faith." Faith does not save and heal. God saves and heals through that open door. You believe, and the power of Christ comes. Salvation and healing are for the glory of God.

PSALMS OF COMFORT

Commit your way to the LORD; *trust also in Him; and He shall bring it to pass.*　　　　　　　　　　　PSALM 37:5

Rest in the LORD, *and wait patiently for Him: fret not yourself because of him who prospers in his way, because of the man who brings wicked devices to pass.*　　　　　　PSALM 37:7

Wait on the LORD, *and keep His way, and He shall exalt you to inherit the land: when the wicked are cut off, you shall see it.*
　　　　　　　　　　　　　　　　　PSALM 37:34

But the salvation of the righteous is of the LORD: *He is their strength in the time of trouble.*　　　　　PSALM 37:39

Blessed is that man that makes the LORD *his trust, and respects not the proud, nor such as turn aside to lies.*　　PSALM 40:4

Why are you cast down, O my soul? and why are you disquieted in me? hope you in God: for I shall yet praise Him for the help of his countenance.　　　　　　　　　　　PSALM 42:5

God is our refuge and strength, a very present help in trouble. Therefore will not we fear, though the earth be removed, and though the mountains be carried into the midst of the sea; though the waters thereof roar and be troubled, though the mountains shake with the swelling thereof. Psalm 46:1–3

Cast your burden upon the Lord, and He shall sustain you: He shall never allow the righteous to be moved. Psalm 55:22

What time I am afraid, I will trust in You. In God I will praise His word, in God I have put my trust; I will not fear what flesh can do to me. Psalm 56:3–4

You shall increase my greatness, and comfort me on every side. Psalm 71:21

In the day of my trouble I sought the Lord: my sore ran in the night, and ceased not: my soul refused to be comforted. Psalm 77:2

I will remember the works of the Lord: surely I will remember Your wonders of old. …Your way is in the sea, and Your path in the great waters, and Your footsteps are not known. Psalm 77:11, 19

Show me a token for good; that they which hate me may see it, and be ashamed: because You, Lord, have helped me, and comforted me.　　　　　　　　　　　　　　　　　　PSALM 86:17

For I have said, Mercy shall be built up for ever: Your faithfulness shall You establish in the very heavens.　　　　PSALM 89:2

In the multitude of my thoughts within me Your comforts delight my soul.　　　　　　　　　　　　　　　　　PSALM 94:19

For as the heaven is high above the earth, so great is His mercy toward them that fear Him.　　　　　　　　PSALM 103:11

He shall not be afraid of evil tidings: his heart is fixed, trusting in the Lord.　　　　　　　　　　　　　　　PSALM 112:7

INSIGHTS ON FAITH FROM SMITH WIGGLESWORTH

Some are anxious because, when they are prayed for, the thing that they are expecting does not happen that same night. They say they believe, but you can see that they are really in turmoil from their unbelief. Abraham believed God. You can hear him saying to Sarah, "Sarah, there is no life in you, and there is nothing in me; but God has promised us a son, and I believe God." That kind of faith is a joy to our Father in heaven.

There are boundless possibilities for us if we dare to act in God and dare to believe that the wonderful power of our living Christ will be made clear through us as we lay our hands on the sick in His name. (See Mark 16:18.)

PSALMS OF COMFORT

Remember the word to Your servant, upon which You have caused me to hope. This is my comfort in my affliction: for Your word has quickened me. The proud have had me greatly in derision: yet have I not declined from Your law. PSALM 119:49–51

I remembered Your judgments of old, O LORD; and have comforted myself. PSALM 119:52

Let, I pray You, Your merciful kindness be for my comfort, according to Your word to Your servant. PSALM 119:76

My eyes fail for Your word, saying, When will You comfort me? PSALM 119:82

They that sow in tears shall reap in joy. PSALM 126:5

I love them that love me; and those that seek me early shall find me. PROVERBS 8:17

DIVINE COMFORT

So I returned, and considered all the oppressions that are done under the sun: and behold the tears of such as were oppressed, and they had no comforter; and on the side of their oppressors there was power; but they had no comforter.　ECCLESIASTES 4:1

And in that day you shall say, O LORD, I will praise You: though You were angry with me, Your anger is turned away, and You comforted me.　ISAIAH 12:1

You will keep him in perfect peace, whose mind is stayed on You: because he trusts in You. Trust you in the LORD for ever: for in the LORD JEHOVAH is everlasting strength.　ISAIAH 26:3–4

And therefore will the LORD wait, that He may be gracious to you, and therefore will He be exalted, that He may have mercy upon you: for the LORD is a God of judgment: blessed are all they that wait for Him.　ISAIAH 30:18

Comfort you, comfort you My people, says your God. Speak you comfortably to Jerusalem, and cry to her, that her warfare is accomplished, that her iniquity is pardoned: for she has received of the LORD's hand double for all her sins.　ISAIAH 40:1–2

The grass withers, the flower fades: but the word of our God shall stand for ever.　ISAIAH 40:8

He shall feed His flock like a shepherd: He shall gather the lambs with his arm, and carry them in His bosom, and shall gently lead those that are with young. Who has measured the waters in the hollow of His hand, and meted out heaven with the span, and comprehended the dust of the earth in a measure, and weighed the mountains in scales, and the hills in a balance? Who has directed the Spirit of the LORD, or being His counsellor has taught him?

ISAIAH 40:11–13

Have you not known? have you not heard, that the everlasting God, the LORD, the Creator of the ends of the earth, faints not, neither is weary? there is no searching of His understanding. He gives power to the faint; and to them that have no might he increases strength.

ISAIAH 40:28–29

He gives power to the faint; and to them that have no might he increases strength. Even the youths shall faint and be weary, and the young men shall utterly fall: but they that wait upon the LORD shall renew their strength; they shall mount up with wings as eagles; they shall run, and not be weary; and they shall walk, and not faint.

ISAIAH 40:29–31

INSIGHTS ON FAITH FROM SMITH WIGGLESWORTH

Are you ready? What for? To be so in the place in which God's Son will be pleased that He gives you all the desires of your heart. Don't forget you are in the presence of God. This day has to be covered with a greater day. It is not what you are; it is what you are intending to be.

～

There are some things in the Scriptures that move me greatly. I am glad that Paul was a human being. I am glad that Jesus became a man. I am glad that Daniel was human, and I am also glad that John was human. You ask, "Why?" Because I see that whatever God has done for other people, He can do for me. And I find that God has done such wonderful things for other people that I am always expecting that these things are possible for me. Think about this. It is a wonderful thought to me.

～

If you want to be healed by the power of God, it means that your life has to be filled with God. We must make sure that the power of God comes to inhabit us. Are you willing to so surrender yourself to God today that Satan will have no dominion over you?

DIVINE COMFORT

Sing, O heavens; and be joyful, O earth; and break forth into singing, O mountains: for the LORD has comforted His people, and will have mercy upon His afflicted.   ISAIAH 49:13

For the LORD shall comfort Zion: He will comfort all her waste places; and He will make her wilderness like Eden, and her desert like the garden of the LORD; joy and gladness shall be found therein, thanksgiving, and the voice of melody.   ISAIAH 51:3

For My thoughts are not your thoughts, neither are your ways My ways, says the LORD. For as the heavens are higher than the earth, so are My ways higher than your ways, and My thoughts than your thoughts.   ISAIAH 55:8–9

As one whom his mother comforts, so will I comfort you; and you shall be comforted in Jerusalem.   ISAIAH 66:13

For he shall be as a tree planted by the waters, and that spreads out her roots by the river, and shall not see when heat comes, but her leaf shall be green; and shall not be careful in the year of drought, neither shall cease from yielding fruit.   JEREMIAH 17:8

The LORD is good to them that wait for Him, to the soul that seeks Him.   LAMENTATIONS 3:25

For the LORD will not cast off for ever: but though He cause grief, yet will He have compassion according to the multitude of His mercies. For He does not afflict willingly nor grieve the children of men.   LAMENTATIONS 3:31–33

Sow to yourselves in righteousness, reap in mercy; break up your fallow ground: for it is time to seek the LORD, till He come and rain righteousness upon you.   HOSEA 10:12

Then the devil leaves Him, and, behold, angels came and ministered to Him.   MATTHEW 4:11

Wherefore, if God so clothe the grass of the field, which to day is, and to morrow is cast into the oven, shall He not much more clothe you, O you of little faith? Therefore take no thought, saying, What shall we eat? or, What shall we drink? or, Wherewithal shall we be clothed? (For after all these things do the Gentiles seek:) for your heavenly Father knows that you have need of all these things.   MATTHEW 6:30–32

If you then, being evil, know how to give good gifts to your children, how much more shall your Father which is in heaven give good things to them that ask Him?   MATTHEW 7:11

But the very hairs of your head are all numbered. Fear you not therefore, you are of more value than many sparrows. Whosoever therefore shall confess Me before men, him will I confess also before My Father which is in heaven. But whosoever shall deny Me before men, him will I also deny before My Father which is in heaven. MATTHEW 10:30–32

And Jesus said to them, Because of your unbelief: for verily I say to you, If you have faith as a grain of mustard seed, you shall say to this mountain, Remove here to yonder place; and it shall remove; and nothing shall be impossible to you. MATTHEW 17:20

Rejoice you in that day, and leap for joy: for, behold, your reward is great in heaven: for in the like manner did their fathers to the prophets. LUKE 6:23

Behold, I give to you power to tread on serpents and scorpions, and over all the power of the enemy: and nothing shall by any means hurt you. LUKE 10:19

INSIGHTS ON FAITH FROM SMITH WIGGLESWORTH

The Lord Himself feed us with the finest of the wheat. He seeks only to bring us into favor with the Father. He says, "Until now you have asked nothing"; ask large things, for my Father and I are one. And as you ask, it will be given you, a measure full, "pressed down, shaken together, and running over," that there will be no leanness in you, but you will be full, overflowing, expressive, God manifest in you, the glory of the Lord upon you, and He bringing forth songs in the earth.

◡

The Lord Jesus is always wanting to show forth His grace and love in order to draw us to Himself. God is willing to do things, to manifest His Word, and to let us know a measure of the mind of our God in this day and hour.

COMFORT PROMISES

Whosoever shall seek to save his life shall lose it; and whosoever shall lose his life shall preserve it. LUKE 17:33

Even the Spirit of truth; whom the world cannot receive, because it sees Him not, neither knows Him: but you know Him; for He dwells with you, and shall be in you. I will not leave you comfortless: I will come to you. JOHN 14:17–18

Peace I leave with you, My peace I give to you: not as the world gives, give I to you. Let not your heart be troubled, neither let it be afraid. JOHN 14:27

And you now therefore have sorrow: but I will see you again, and your heart shall rejoice, and your joy no man take from you. JOHN 16:22

But the Comforter, which is the Holy Ghost, whom the Father will send in My name, He shall teach you all things, and bring all things to your remembrance, whatsoever I have said to you. JOHN 14:26

Confirming the souls of the disciples, and exhorting them to continue in the faith, and that we must through much tribulation enter into the kingdom of God. ACTS 14:22

And the brethren immediately sent away Paul and Silas by night to Berea: who coming there went into the synagogue of the Jews. These were more noble than those in Thessalonica, in that they received the word with all readiness of mind, and searched the scriptures daily, whether those things were so.   ACTS 17:10–11

Likewise the Spirit also helps our infirmities: for we know not what we should pray for as we ought: but the Spirit itself makes intercession for us with groanings which cannot be uttered. And he that searches the hearts knows what is the mind of the Spirit, because he makes intercession for the saints according to the will of God. And we know that all things work together for good to them that love God, to them who are the called according to His purpose.   ROMANS 8:26–28

He that spared not His own Son, but delivered Him up for us all, how shall He not with Him also freely give us all things?

ROMANS 8:32

For I am persuaded, that neither death, nor life, nor angels, nor principalities, nor powers, nor things present, nor things to come, nor height, nor depth, nor any other creature, shall be able to separate us from the love of God, which is in Christ Jesus our Lord.

ROMANS 8:38–39

O the depth of the riches both of the wisdom and knowledge of God! how unsearchable are His judgments, and His ways past finding out! For who has known the mind of the Lord? or who has been His counsellor? Or who has first given to Him, and it shall be recompensed to Him again? For of Him, and through Him, and to Him, are all things: to whom be glory for ever. Amen.

ROMANS 11:33–36

Now the God of hope fill you with all joy and peace in believing, that you may abound in hope, through the power of the Holy Ghost.   ROMANS 15:13

What? know you not that your body is the temple of the Holy Ghost which is in you, which you have of God, and you are not your own? For you are bought with a price: therefore glorify God in your body, and in your spirit, which are God's.

1 CORINTHIANS 6:19–20

INSIGHTS ON FAITH FROM SMITH WIGGLESWORTH

The Bible is full of entreaty for you to come and partake and receive the grace, the power, the strength, the righteousness, and the full redemption of Jesus Christ. He never fails to hear when we believe. This same Jesus is in our midst to touch and to free you.

～

Around the pool of Bethesda lay a great multitude of sick folk—blind, lame, paralyzed—waiting for the moving of the water. (See John 5:2–4.) Did Jesus heal all of them? No, He left many around that pool unhealed. Undoubtedly, many had their eyes on the pool and had no eyes for Jesus. There are many today who always have their confidence in things they can see. If they would only get their eyes on God instead of on natural things, how quickly they would be helped.

COMFORT PROMISES

Blessed be God, even the Father of our Lord Jesus Christ, the Father of mercies, and the God of all comfort; who comforts us in all our tribulation, that we may be able to comfort them which are in any trouble, by the comfort wherewith we ourselves are comforted of God. 2 CORINTHIANS 1:3–4

For as the sufferings of Christ abound in us, so our consolation also abounds by Christ. And whether we be afflicted, it is for your consolation and salvation, which is effectual in the enduring of the same sufferings which we also suffer: or whether we be comforted, it is for your consolation and salvation. And our hope of you is steadfast, knowing, that as you are partakers of the sufferings, so shall you be also of the consolation. 2 CORINTHIANS 1:5–7

We are troubled on every side, yet not distressed; we are perplexed, but not in despair; persecuted, but not forsaken; cast down, but not destroyed. 2 CORINTHIANS 4:8–9

And He said to me, My grace is sufficient for you: for My strength is made perfect in weakness. Most gladly therefore will I rather glory in my infirmities, that the power of Christ may rest upon me. Therefore I take pleasure in infirmities, in reproaches, in necessities, in persecutions, in distresses for Christ's sake: for when I am weak, then am I strong. 2 CORINTHIANS 12:9–10

This I say then, Walk in the Spirit, and you shall not fulfill the lust of the flesh. GALATIANS 5:16

But the fruit of the Spirit is love, joy, peace, longsuffering, gentleness, goodness, faith, meekness, temperance: against such there is no law. GALATIANS 5:22–23

Finally, my brethren, be strong in the Lord, and in the power of His might. EPHESIANS 6:10

Finally, brethren, whatsoever things are true, whatsoever things are honest, whatsoever things are just, whatsoever things are pure, whatsoever things are lovely, whatsoever things are of good report; if there be any virtue, and if there be any praise, think on these things. PHILIPPIANS 4:8

I can do all things through Christ which strengthens me. PHILIPPIANS 4:13

But my God shall supply all your need according to His riches in glory by Christ Jesus. PHILIPPIANS 4:19

Who has delivered us from the power of darkness, and has translated us into the kingdom of His dear Son. COLOSSIANS 1:13

Who will have all men to be saved, and to come to the knowledge of the truth. For there is one God, and one mediator between God and men, the man Christ Jesus. 1 TIMOTHY 2:4–5

You therefore, my son, be strong in the grace that is in Christ Jesus. 2 TIMOTHY 2:1

For we have great joy and consolation in your love, because the bowels of the saints are refreshed by you, brother.
PHILEMON 1:7

Are they not all ministering spirits, sent forth to minister for them who shall be heirs of salvation? HEBREWS 1:14

And God shall wipe away all tears from their eyes; and there shall be no more death, neither sorrow, nor crying, neither shall there be any more pain: for the former things are passed away.
REVELATION 21:4

INSIGHTS ON FAITH FROM SMITH WIGGLESWORTH

God is gracious and is *"not willing that any should perish"* (2 Peter 3:9). How many are willing to make a clean break from their sins? I tell you that the moment you do this, God will open heaven. It is an easy thing for Him to save your soul and heal your disease if you will only come and take shelter today in *"the secret place of the Most High"* (Psalm 91:1).

If you know it is scriptural for you to be healed of every weakness, never rest until God makes the healing yours. If you know that the Scriptures teach holiness, purity, and divine likeness—overcoming under all conditions—never rest until you are an overcomer.

Where absolute weakness is, so that you feel you cannot stand the trial, God comes in and enables you to stand. Life is ministered to you; Christ takes the place of weakness. You can say, *"When I am weak, then am I strong"* (2 Corinthians 12:10), for God touches you with His strength.

COMFORT VICTORY

Looking to Jesus the author and finisher of our faith; who for the joy that was set before Him endured the cross, despising the shame, and is set down at the right hand of the throne of God.
HEBREWS 12:2

My brethren, count it all joy when you fall into divers temptations; knowing this, that the trying of your faith works patience.
JAMES 1:2–3

If any of you lack wisdom, let him ask of God, that gives to all men liberally, and upbraids not; and it shall be given him. But let him ask in faith, nothing wavering. For he that wavers is like a wave of the sea driven with the wind and tossed. For let not that man think that he shall receive any thing of the Lord. A double minded man is unstable in all his ways.
JAMES 1:5–8

Blessed is the man that endures temptation: for when he is tried, he shall receive the crown of life, which the Lord has promised to them that love Him.
JAMES 1:12

Behold, we count them happy which endure. You have heard of the patience of Job, and have seen the end of the Lord; that the Lord is very pitiful, and of tender mercy.
JAMES 5:11

Wherein you greatly rejoice, though now for a season, if need be, you are in heaviness through manifold temptations. 1 PETER 1:6

But if we walk in the light, as He is in the light, we have fellowship one with another, and the blood of Jesus Christ His Son cleanses us from all sin. 1 JOHN 1:7

By which also He went and preached to the spirits in prison. 1 PETER 3:19

Beloved, think it not strange concerning the fiery trial which is to try you, as though some strange thing happened to you: but rejoice, inasmuch as you are partakers of Christ's sufferings; that, when His glory shall be revealed, you may be glad also with exceeding joy. 1 PETER 4:12–13

Casting all your care upon him; for He cares for you. 1 PETER 5:7

But the God of all grace, who has called us to His eternal glory by Christ Jesus, after that you have suffered a while, make you perfect, stablish, strengthen, settle you. 1 PETER 5:10

In this was manifested the love of God toward us, because that God sent His only begotten Son into the world, that we might live through Him. Herein is love, not that we loved God, but that He loved us, and sent His Son to be the propitiation for our sins.

1 JOHN 4:9–10

These things have I written to you that believe on the name of the Son of God; that you may know that you have eternal life, and that you may believe on the name of the Son of God.

1 JOHN 5:13

Grace be with you, mercy, and peace, from God the Father, and from the Lord Jesus Christ, the Son of the Father, in truth and love.

2 JOHN 1:3

Beloved, I wish above all things that you may prosper and be in health, even as your soul prospers.

3 JOHN 1:2

"GOD IS WAITING FOR PEOPLE WHO DARE TO BELIEVE, AND WHEN YOU BELIEVE, 'ALL THINGS ARE POSSIBLE' (MARK 9:23). ONLY BELIEVE, ONLY BELIEVE; ALL THINGS ARE POSSIBLE, ONLY BELIEVE. ONLY BELIEVE, ONLY BELIEVE; ALL THINGS ARE POSSIBLE, ONLY BELIEVE. GOD WANTS TO SWEEP AWAY ALL UNBELIEF FROM YOUR HEART. HE WANTS YOU TO DARE TO BELIEVE HIS WORD."

—SMITH WIGGLESWORTH

The Smith Wigglesworth quotes throughout this book were taken from the following Whitaker House published titles…

Smith Wigglesworth on Faith
978-0-88368-531-0

> Faith is a gift of God that is available to all who will receive it.

Smith Wigglesworth: The Power of Faith
978-0-88368-608-9

> The sustaining effect of the smallest drop of faith will create continual ripples of power.

Smith Wigglesworth on Ever Increasing Faith
978-0-88368-633-1

> Join the evangelist in the great adventure called "faith."

Smith Wigglesworth on the Power of Scripture
978-1-60374-094-4

> You will cherish this glimpse into the heart and mind of one of God's most gifted servants.

Smith Wigglesworth on the Anointing
978-0-88368-530-3

> As you live in His anointing, your spiritual life will become more fruitful.

Smith Wigglesworth on the Holy Spirit
978-0-88368-544-0

> Learn how the fullness of the Holy Spirit can be yours.

Smith Wigglesworth on Healing
978-0-88368-426-9

> Not only can you be healed of your sicknesses, but God can use you to bring healing to others.

Smith Wigglesworth on Spiritual Gifts
978-0-88368-533-4

> You can be the instrument God uses to transmit His love and miracles to others.

Smith Wigglesworth on Heaven
978-0-88368-954-7

> Discover God's plans for you in this life and what He has in store for you in the heaven.

The beloved, classic KJV text with its language updated to modern equivalents without any doctrinal changes.

In this translation, the trusted KJV text remains doctrinally intact, but its archaic language and difficult words have been replaced for clarity with their modern equivalents.

This Bible is also a complete red letter edition, meaning that the direct words of God are indicated in red in both the Old and New Testaments–currently the only Bible with this feature.

If you want to pass along the KJV that you know and love to the next generation of believers without compromising the translation that you trust, the KJVER is the Bible for you.

The Trusted King James in an Easy Read Format ™

whitakerhouse.com/kjver